Foundations for
SPIRITUAL GROWTH
Building on God's Word

Foundations for
SPIRITUAL GROWTH
Building on God's Word

ROGER W. F. SKEPPLE

EDEN BOOK PRESS • MORROW GEORGIA

EDEN BOOK PRESS
2178 Morrow, Georgia
30260, USA

Unless otherwise noted, Scripture taken from the *New American Standard Bible*, © 1960, 1962, 1963, 1968, 1871, 1972, 1973, 1975, 1977, by The Lockman Foundation. Used by permission.

ISBN 978-0-9660562-7-3
Suggested Subject Heading: Christian Living, Theology, Doctrinal Studies, Spiritual Growth

© 1995, 2018
Revised Edition; Roger W. F. Skepple. All rights reserved.
Printed in the United States of America.

Cover Design: Joseph E. Banks

No part of this book may be reproduced without written permission, except for brief quotations in books and critical reviews.

I dedicate this book to two very important men,
who have profoundly affected my life.
My father, Adolphus D. Skepple, who refused to let me
wander from the Lord, although I tried,
and my father-in-law, Starling J. Hopkins Jr.,
who accepted me into his home as his own son,
and whose advice has stood the test of time.

Acknowledgments

A number of years ago I started a journey to develop a lay training program to equip lay men and women in the Bible and theology, so that they might be able to teach others. Spurred on by the belief that lay men and women could understand and communicate God's Word as effectively as institutionally trained persons, having witnessed such in my own father and father-in-law, the lay training program entitled the Titus Project was born. The name Titus was chosen because of the challenge Titus faced of ministering in his context, a challenge that all ministry possesses. *Foundations for Spiritual Growth* is just a small portion of the fruit of this effort.

I must acknowledge two groups of men who have allowed me the privilege of leading and guiding them in their spiritual development. To Elliott Greene, who taught with me early on in the process, and to Sling Patterson, who later took over as my co-teacher. To Les Jackson, the lone survivor of our early efforts and a faithful teacher of God's Word and to Leroy Harrison, Alfred Johnson, Tommy King, Anthony McClanahan,

David Sheppard, and Clint Thomas, who made up the first full graduating class.

Two other very important men who have influenced the development of this book must also be mentioned. Pastor Warren Mattox, who early in my efforts, encouraged me to not just write on theology, but to go one step further and give practical application based upon it. Also, Pastor Larry Mercer, who instilled in me by his example, the need to be absolutely relevant and practical, while remaining thoroughly Biblical.

A final word of thanks must be given to my wife, Teresa, who assisted me in the editing of the manuscript for this book.

I would be remiss to fail to mention the crucial role another individual played in the publishing of this book. Not only did he encourage me to pursue publishing but walked me through the steps necessary to do such. For this I would like to extend a gracious thank you to LaFayette Holland, a true friend indeed.

For this, the second edition of *Foundations*, I would like to personally thank Rachel Robinson and Ken Simmons for their editing and suggestions, as well as Rachel's work on cleaning up the manuscript for publication.

Table of Contents

Preface.. 11

Part One ♦ The Basics
Foundational Truths of Spiritual Growth

1. Passages of Growth: An Introduction to Spiritual Growth. 17
2. The Holy Scriptures. 41
3. The Godhead.. 51

Part Two ♦ God's Handiwork
The Creation of Angels and Man and Their Implication for Spiritual Growth

4. The Existence and Role of Angelic Beings. 65
5. The Origin and Nature of Mankind.. 83

Part Three ♦ God's Salvation
Sin, Christ, Salvation, and the Spirit and Their Implications for Spiritual Growth

6. The Nature, Types, and Cure of Sin. 99
7. The Person and Work of Jesus Christ. 115

| 8. | The Basis and Means of Salvation............ | 127 |
| 9. | The Holy Spirit............................ | 145 |

Part Four ♦ God's Summation
The Church and the End Times and Their Implications for Spiritual Growth

| 10. | The Church............................... | 159 |
| 11. | The End Times and the Eternal State........... | 179 |

Appendices

Appendix One: The Bible's Authenticity. 197
Appendix Two: Overcoming Common Weaknesses..... 203
Appendix Three: Study and Devotions. 207
Appendix Four: Overcoming Hindrances. 215
Appendix Five: Assurance of Salvation. 219
Appendix Six: Dodging Distractions.................. 221
Appendix Seven: Postscript on the Holy Spirit......... 225

Works Cited. 247
Endnotes.. 249

Preface

Spiritual growth is something that many Christians talk about, but few know how to accomplish in their own lives or the lives of others. Growth in the spiritual realm of our existence was not something that God wanted us to either guess about or to be unsure of. Every believer has the capacity for spiritual growth within themselves, in much the same way that they possess the capacity for physical growth. In the realm of physical growth, each child who is born into the world is placed on a continuum that will eventually lead them to adulthood. With the proper nourishment, both physical (food) and emotional (love), care, and time, that child will inevitably become a well balanced adult. This process is due to the nature of physical birth. A child will become an adult given the above factors.

Our spiritual birth is much the same way. God has given the believer new birth. At that new birth, God gives to the believer a seed which will inevitably produce a spiritual adult (cf. 1 Jn. 3:9). However, just as with physical growth, so it is with spiritual growth. Without the proper nourishment, abnormal things will occur. For the believer, that nourishment comes essentially in three forms: the Word of God, interpersonal relationships, and suffering. Without these three elements effectively manifesting themselves to and through the believer's life, abnormal or stunted growth will occur. The primary component of the process is the Word of God itself, because it sets the tone for the believer's response to the other two crucial areas and tells him how to properly conduct himself through them. The focus of this particular work is to investigate this first form of nourishment to the believer's life, which is the Word of God.

Now there are a number of approaches that could be adopted to accomplish this task. However, a particular biblical model will be adopted for this work, that of the New Testament Epistle. When the New Testament writers wrote, in order to both fix error or encourage continuance in growth, they always began with sound doctrine. From this foundation of sound doctrine they moved on to the sphere of application. In this section they showed how the doctrinal truths they had just explained were then worked out in the world here and now. This process effectively brought into play three of the crucial aspects to man's existence: his mind, will, and emotions. The writers first informed the believer's mind as to what the truth was. They then motivated the will through exhortation to perform the truth. Finally, as believers began living the truth in their daily lives, their emotions were engaged in support of their lifestyle.

Taking this basic structure, *Foundations of Spiritual Growth* will offer a comprehensive **beginning** course in doctrine with a heavy emphasis on personal appropriation of that doctrine into one's personal life. Ten crucial doctrines will be studied and some of their implications for the Christian's life will be expounded. Also included in this work is a historical perspective on the doctrines affirmed throughout. This is accomplished through an opening excerpt from one of the many doctrinal statements or affirmations that have been written by the church throughout its almost two thousand years of existence. This allows the believer to have a clear view on beliefs of the church throughout the ages.

The following list will give the reader some insight into what the *Foundations of Spiritual Growth* should accomplish in their lives:

A. Relative to Apprehension
1. That the reader will come to understand that the lifelong study of the Bible and theology is vital to his faith, that is, his Christianity and his growth as a believer.
2. That the reader will gain the required knowledge to understand and be conversant with the foundational doctrines of Scripture and Christianity.
3. That the reader will gain insight into the interrelationship between having a growing relationship with God and thinking rightly about God.
4. That the reader will acquire the ability to think intelligently about his faith and the Bible.

B. **Relative to Attitude**
1. That the reader will be encouraged as he realizes that the Bible can be understood and applied, and thus gain the results about which it talks.
2. That the reader will be spiritually enriched by a study of God and His relationship to His creation.
3. That the reader will be sobered by a deeper understanding of the God he serves.
4. That the reader will have a greater appreciation for the Word and his walk with God.

C. **Relative to Action**
1. That the reader will be able to take the principles taught in this book and apply them to his life in a distinctive and personal manner.
2. That the reader will propel himself into a more intimate walk with his Savior through the interaction of the Word and the Holy Spirit.
3. That the reader will add those godly virtues that the Scriptures indicate ought to be a part of every believer's continual growth.
4. That the reader will gain assurance in his walk with God.

Part One
♦
The Basics

Foundational Truths of
Spiritual Growth

Chapter One
PASSAGES OF GROWTH
An Introduction to Spiritual Growth

The Christian life is a multifaceted life. There are a number of important passageways that will lead the Christian to spiritual growth. The focus of this chapter is to look at just a few of the important elements necessary for our growth as Christians. It is not meant to be exhaustive but succinct and to the point about our spiritual growth as believers. First we will look at the mandate for growth.

The Mandate for Spiritual Growth
The biblical mandate on the believer's life for growth is found in John 15:1-6, which is part of the broader context of John 15:1-11. This passage of Scripture is found in what is referred to as the Upper Room Discourse. The Upper Room Discourse, which extends from John 13 through John 17, is Jesus' last extended teaching moment with His disciples before

His crucifixion. As such, its importance to the Christian's life is clearly apparent. In it we have the heart of Jesus' instruction for His disciples. In order to properly understand 15:1-6 an understanding of the preceding context is important. The following is a brief outline of the preceding passages.

13:1-20	Discusses the importance of humility
13:21-30	Tells of the removal of Judas
13:31-14:31	Expounds on Jesus being the only way to the Father (14:6)
13:31-38	Deals with the fact that He is going
14:1-6	Indicates where He is going
14:7-15	Tells why He is going—why He is the only way to get to where He is going
14:16-31	How the disciples will be able to follow—the Holy Spirit

John 15:1-6 is one of the most difficult passages in the Bible to understand. As such, a careful study of it will be needed, if we are to properly understand and apply it. The difficulty lies in the fact that the branch, or person, that seems to be in Christ (15:2), but does not produce fruit is burned up (15:6). How does this align with eternal security? The first issue we must realize before we look at the passage is that the Bible clearly teaches that the believer is eternally secure. That is, once a person is saved, he is always saved, or in other words, God completes what He starts. For clearer amplification of this point and Biblical support, the reader should look to appendix

five. With this fact in mind it is possible to now look at John 15.

John 15:1 gives us the source of growth in the believer's life. Growth does not happen independent of the vine. When you cut a branch off from the vine it does not grow, it cannot grow. Therefore, it is only in being properly connected to the vine that proper growth can take place. It is also important to notice that even the producer/catalyst of the growth is not the branch, but the vinedresser, who is God. He is the one who takes responsibility for growth. A vinedresser is the person who guides and manages the growth of the vine. Likewise, it is God who guides and directs the growth of the believer's life (cf. Phil. 2:12-13). Any good vinedresser makes sure that the plant, for which He is caring, has the proper nutrients and fertilizer, as well as the proper amounts of water and sunshine. He must also take into account the growth of the individual parts of the plant, and make the necessary adjustments to the plant regarding its growth. This last point serves as a good transition to the next verse.

15:2 contrasts two different branches, one bears fruit and the other does not. In this verse, we will be focusing upon the branch that bears fruit and the branch that does not bear fruit will be addressed in 15:6, where it is once again described and analyzed. It says of the one who bears fruit, that he is pruned for the purpose of bearing more fruit. Pruning is a very important part of the vinedresser's work. If proper growth in the vine is to be maintained, parts of the vine, which are unnecessarily absorbing the needed nutrients, must be removed.

Therefore, dead branches, which are still fed by the trunk of the vine, must be cut off so that nutrients will not be wasted. Also, unnecessary foliage must also be pruned from the healthy branches, so that they can continue to effectively grow at an even greater rate and capacity. This process is the same with the believer. Growth is not a one time occurrence in the believer's life, but an ongoing process controlled by God. Notice that God has the pruning shears, not us. God is the one who decides what must be cut, not us. God chooses the time, not us. You will be pruned whether you like (or want) it or not. In the life of the believer, growth is not an option.

The implicit comparison which Jesus has been making in these first two verses between the vine\branch relationship and the Jesus/disciple relationship now becomes explicit in 15:3. The third verse in this passage declares that the disciples are already clean. The word translated "clean" in this verse has the same root word as that which is translated "prunes" in the previous verse. Jesus is demonstrating that the disciples are in a state of being pruned. God has and is pruning them in order to accrue greater amounts of growth from them. This brings up the issue of Judas however. Is he included in the "you" of this verse? From Jesus' statement in John 13:6-11, we know that he was not included.

In 13:6-11, Jesus is giving instruction on humility. He demonstrates the greatest show of humility by washing the feet of the disciples. Since the Teacher and Lord washed the feet of the disciples, how much more should they respond in like manner to each other (13:13-17)? While washing the disciples' feet, Jesus is prohibited by Peter from washing his. Jesus makes it clear that such a washing was a testimony to being His own (13:8). Peter then makes the brash statement that he wants Jesus to wash all of him. In answering Peter, Jesus indicates that once "completely clean" one only needs to wash his feet. This spoke of the ultimate forgiveness given by Christ and after salvation occurs, only needs to be augmented by confession of daily sin. In this verse Jesus makes the following statement, "and you are clean, but not all *of you*"(13:10). This is a statement of exclusion of the one betraying Him (13:11). These verses provide the verbal link between chapter thirteen and fifteen. The same word clean used in fifteen, which is the root of the word prune, is the same word Jesus uses for clean in chapter thirteen. His usage of clean, however, excludes Judas. The fact that Judas is excluded is also affirmed in 13:18-19. However, even up to chapter fifteen, the disciples are still believing that Judas is included as indicated by John 13:29-30. So when these statements are taken in light of the defection of Judas, they are properly understood as a statement of the identification of true believers. When looking back on Jesus' words about the vine and the branches, they will know that Judas was not clean, and therefore was not one of the branches that bore fruit. Although he seemed like he bore fruit and appeared to be in the vine, he actually was not.

The next two verses, 15:4-5, are quite forceful about the source and means of growth. Jesus states the source of growth quite emphatically when He says, "the branch cannot bear fruit of itself . . . apart from Me you can do nothing" (vv. 4c, 5e).

The means of growth is abiding in Christ. No growth can take place outside of Christ, and as such for growth to occur the believer must remain in Christ. This again speaks to the issue of Judas. Although he seemed like he was a branch who was in Christ and would have confessed to be so, he actually was not abiding in Christ, but masquerading as a believer, and therefore was not bringing forth real fruit (cf. 1 Jn. 2:18-26). This naturally leads into the second branch that we did not discuss under 15:2. The branch that does not bear fruit.

The unfruitful branch/person is again mentioned here in 15:6. His fate is that he is cast away and burned up with fire. Is this a believer or an unsaved person? There are several reasons for considering this person as an unsaved person. First, in the broader context, Jesus is giving His instruction in the context of Judas' defection. As noted earlier, there are verbal ties between this chapter and chapter thirteen, in which Jesus clearly lays out the fact of Judas' exclusion, but in veiled terms. Upon later investigation, the disciples, when combining Christ's veiled terms in chapter thirteen and His clear pronouncements in chapter fifteen, with the facts of what Judas did, would clearly be able to make the conclusion that he was the branch that did not bring forth real fruit, although seemingly in Christ. How does this connect with what seems to be the affirmation that the branch is in Christ? This leads to the second issue.

The prepositional phrase "in Me" is used six times in this chapter. In those six cases, grammatically, it has the potential of being either an adjectival phrase or adverbial. In five of the six cases it can only be adverbial (15:4-7). In the sixth case, which is the first occurrence, it could either be adjectival (modifying "branch") or adverbial (modifying "bear fruit"). Each option has a different meaning. If it is adjectival it would mean every Christian and would properly be translated, "Every branch in Me." If it was adverbial, it would refer to the context of fruit bearing itself and would properly be translated, "Every branch that does not bear fruit in Me." Our English translations are not helpful at this point, because they attempt to render the emphasis of the Greek text not the sense of the passage. You see, in the Greek language they did not have an unbending word order to communicate grammatical relationships as we do in the English language. As such, words were flexible and could appear anywhere in the sentence because their grammatical markers were part of the word itself. If an author wanted to emphasize a particular word or concept, he would move that word to the very front of the sentence. The phrase "in Me" appears at the very front of the sentence, therefore its grammatical relationship must be made by way of interpretation, since it could be modifying either branch or bear fruit. Contextually, given the fact of Judas and that every other usage of this phrase is adverbial, the best option is to take the phrase "in Me" of 15:2 to be adverbial and not adjectival. As such it tells us nothing of the true nature of this branch, just what the branch is not doing, which is "bearing fruit in Christ."

Third, Jesus promised believers that He would not cast them away in John 6:37. This term "cast away" in John 6:37 is the same term used in 15:6 which is translated "thrown away".

Jesus could not make the statement in 6:37 that He would not throw away believers and then in 15:6 say that He would throw them away. That is contradictory. These cannot be real believers.

Fourth, nowhere in the Bible does God say that the believer will be burned. While their works may be burned with fire (1 Cor. 3:10-15), they themselves are never imaged as being burned with fire. So this is clearly a person who looked like he was abiding, but was actually out (cf. 1 Jn. 2:19). In this context, fruit bearing is the love produced in the believer for God and other believers by the indwelling of Christ in the believer's life.

So what might be concluded from this passage of Scripture regarding spiritual growth? It is not an option. Spiritual growth is a mandate from God. It is something that happens to true believers. In saying this however, it is important to note that even in John 15 Christ recognized that there were levels of fruitfulness. 15:2 indicates that the branch bears fruit. God prunes it so that it would bear **more** fruit. Christ's ultimate goal is that they would bear **much** fruit. So here we see that there are at least three different levels of fruitfulness enunciated. Everyone is not at the same level, nor are they growing at the same rate, but true believers grow. We must therefore become serious about our own growth in Christ. As noted earlier, God is the Vinedresser and therefore sees about such growth taking place. Christ said in 15:8 that when we grow we "prove" ourselves to be His disciples, not to Him or the Father, who already know our true identity, but rather to ourselves and others (cf. Jam. 2:14-26).

Fertilizer for Spiritual Growth

Next we will turn from The Mandate For Spiritual Growth to The Fertilizer of Spiritual Growth. Here we will be concerned with some of the important processes which God uses to propel his people to growth. Although God has the pruning shears, John 15 also tells us that He is the Vinedresser (John 15:1). As the Vinedresser, God supplies the fertilizer and growth supplements to stimulate the production of fruit. We will look at five of the most important types of fertilizer that God uses to ensure the growth of His people. They are: 1) hardship; 2) encouragement; 3) accountability; 4) time; and 5) humility. These growth supplements will be looked at through the lenses of biblical characters who exhibited these characteristics and thus grew to bear fruit.

Hardship

The story of Joseph is one that stretches from Genesis 37 through Genesis 50. It is a story of much tribulation and hardship. However, the one distinguishing mark that stands out more than anything else in the story of his life is the fact that throughout these afflictions he maintained a divine perspective. When we first meet Joseph, he is in a situation, because of the favoritism shown him by his father Jacob, where he is hated by his siblings. In the midst of this dilemma, however, God relates to Joseph through two dreams that he is in fact the one chosen from the family to be the vehicle of divine interaction (Genesis 37:1-11). His family responds negatively to the dreams, and it ultimately leads to him being sold into slavery by his jealous brothers and then taken to Egypt (Gen. 37:8, 10-36).

The story of Joseph does not pick up again until Genesis 39, in which we have the account of Joseph and Potiphar's wife. Joseph, who was doing very well in Egypt because of God's blessing, was put in charge of all of Potiphar's goods (39:1-6). However, when a plot to seduce Joseph by Potiphar's wife failed, she lied about it and had him thrown in jail (39:7-20).

The interesting thing about the story at this juncture is that we have no indication that God had revealed to Joseph that He would be taking care of Him in Egypt, and making him prosper. However, when he is confronted by Potiphar's wife, his defense is that he cannot commit adultery with her because such would be sin in God's eyes (39:9). Even in the face of a difficult situation, Joseph maintained a divine perspective. So much so that by the end of the book of Genesis, when summing up the goal of his brothers in attempting to kill him, he makes this statement, "And as for you, you meant evil against me, **but** God meant it for good in order to bring about this present result, to preserve many people alive" (50:20). Throughout his life, he focused not upon his circumstances, but upon his God.

Encouragement and Accountability

Encouragement and accountability are two of the most powerful supplements for growth in the believer's life. A clear illustration of the power of encouragement and accountability is that of Barnabas. His very name meant "Son of Encouragement" (Acts 4:36). Every glimpse of his life that we have in the New Testament shows him encouraging and building up others. In Acts 4:36-37 he sells a portion of property which he owned, in order to provide for the needs of the Jerusalem believers. The next mention of Barnabas is in Acts 9. In this chapter Paul, the famous persecutor of the church, is converted to Jesus Christ (9:1-19), and immediately begins to preach Christ, first in Damascus, where he was saved, and then in Jerusalem (9:19-26). However, while in Jerusalem he is understandably shunned by the believers, until Barnabas reached out his hand to him (9:27-30). Barnabas again shows up in Acts 11. In this chapter, the church at Jerusalem spreads out due to persecution and while its members are fleeing, they witness and begin to make an impact in Gentile territory, namely Antioch (11:19-21). The one chosen to go and see to the Gentiles' growth is not one of the apostles, but rather Barnabas (11:22), who takes care "to encourage them all with a resolute heart to remain true to the Lord" (11:23). For help he enlists Paul, probably ushering him, into his first local church ministry (11:24-26). During this time he and Paul took help from Antioch to famine stricken Jerusalem to help the believers there (11:27-30; 12:25). He is always seen encouraging others.

Shortly following the famine visit, Barnabas and Paul set out on the first missionary journey to take the gospel to other regions of the known world (13:1-14:28). Upon their return, they are sent by the church of Antioch to defend the idea that Gentiles do not have to take on the legalistic tenets of Judaism in order to be saved (15:1-35). The last mention of Barnabas in the book of Acts is found in 15:36-41. At this point, he and Paul part company over Barnabas' nephew John Mark. Mark had deserted them during their first journey and Paul did not want to take him along again (13:13; 15:38). As a result, Barnabas and Paul separated ways, Barnabas taking Mark and Paul taking Silas (15:39-41). Although he does not appear again in the book of Acts, Barnabas' affect can be felt beyond its pages. In Colossians 4:10 Mark has so matured under Barnabas' encouraging hand that years later Paul can suggest him as one of the few encouragements in his life. Barnabas' legacy of encouragement has been passed on so effectively that in the last letter Paul writes, before he is killed for the cause of Christ, he requests that Mark comes to serve him (2 Tim. 4:11). Through Barnabas' encouragement and accountable relationship with John Mark, Mark developed into a mighty servant of the Lord.

Time and Humility

The last two growth supplements to be addressed are illustrated in the life of Moses. Moses' life demonstrates that both time and humility are important if we are going to grow as we should as Christians. Moses' life is one of a rise to a position of prestige, to a fall when he fled for Midian, and then to a rise again as the leader of God's people. His story begins in Exodus 2. Moses was born at a time when the nation of Israel was in bondage in Egypt. Exodus 1 records the rise of a Pharaoh (which means king) who was not familiar with the life and times of Joseph, who had found great favor in the eyes of the Egyptians (1:1-8). A fear of the Jews spread at that time because of their great numbers, and resulted in the Egyptians placing the Jews in harsh forced labor (1:9-14). By doing this they hoped to control their growth in numbers. When this did not work, they tried to kill all the male children, which was circumvented by the Jewish midwives (1:15-22). It was in this context that Moses was born. Having been born and protected by his mother as long as possible, it finally came to a point where he had to be made known (2:1-3). He was hid in a basket and set adrift on the Nile, where he was discovered by the Pharaoh's daughter, and eventually raised as Pharaoh's son (2:3-10). However, Moses never forgot his heritage, because he was cared for by his mother (2:9).

When Moses was grown, he witnessed an Egyptian beating one of his countrymen and killed the Egyptian in secret, or so he thought (2:11-12). However, the incident was not unobserved and Moses fled from Egypt in fear of his life (2:13-22). No doubt he was disillusioned. He probably thought he was ready to move in and free his people, but the very people he wanted to help rejected him (2:14).

Over the next forty years, the cry of the people because of their hard labor increased and got worse, reaching the point that God would move on their behalf to bring about freedom (2:23-25). When God is ready to free the people from their bondage, it is Moses that He calls upon (3:1-9). The Moses, who was so quick to help out then, is not so quick to help out now (3:10-4:17). Moses had learned some important lessons.

He spent forty years in the desert learning humility and patience. God used this extended time in his life to give him a proper perspective on himself. While he went away an impetuous young man, he came back a patient man (he patiently endured the children of Israel's disobedience in the wilderness). While he went away an independent young man, he came back a dependent man (dependence on God throughout the exodus out of Egypt). He went away a proud young man, he came back a humble man (3:11). God used time and humility to produce one of His most important leaders.

When God uses the fertilizers of hardship, encouragement, accountability, time, and humility, the growth of His people is imminent.

The Building Blocks of Spiritual Growth

Having dealt with the Fertilizers of Spiritual Growth, it is now time to focus upon the Building Blocks of Spiritual Growth. These building blocks are important to the Christian's general growth and maturity in the Lord. It is these particular virtues that provide the believer with an ample basis upon which he can effectively participate with the Spirit in fostering his own growth. The concept of building blocks communicates the idea of what is foundational and necessary, and the following three virtues are just that. These virtues are faith, hope, and love. Each are difficult to establish, but once properly stationed in our lives, are sturdy supports for our spiritual maturation.

Faith/Contentment

There are many possible avenues to travel in attempting to discuss the virtue of faith. A different approach would be to investigate faith from its subsidiary virtue, that of contentment. The passage of Scripture from which we are going to explore contentment is Matthew chapter six. This chapter falls in what is titled the Sermon on the Mount which stretches from Matthew 5:1-7:29. In this prolonged discourse, Jesus teaches on the kingdom and how the Kingdom Dweller is to conduct himself in the world. Chapter six may be divided into two distinct yet related parts. 6:1-18 discusses the *Practice of the Kingdom Dweller* and 6:19-34 discusses the *Faith of the Kingdom Dweller*.

Jesus' focus in chapter six is on an interior religion that works itself out, rather than a purely exterior one. Notice what 6:1 indicates. Because the Pharisees had an exterior religion, they sought immediate exterior rewards for it. Jesus set a whole new standard. Practice your righteousness not before man but before God. These three acts (alms, prayer and fasting) are not the only things that can be practiced on the exterior, of course, but Jesus picked three of the most important works in Judaism, thus emphasizing His point.

Jesus deals with the issue of contentment by setting it in contrast to anxiety. The first statement Jesus makes about anxiety is that to cure it you must place your treasure where you want your heart to be (6:19-21). There will be no victory over anxiety, as long as you are content to work only for the goods and benefits of this world. There is a song that claims to interpret this passage and it simply says "where your heart is there is your treasure also." This however is only half true. It is not where you set your heart, but where you set your treasure, those things which you find important and essential.

Jesus' second statement in this regard is that of service (6:22-24). Who is it that you serve? Mixed loyalties or divided allegiances cause havoc and confusion in the believer's life. It is impossible for one to serve two masters. When one tries to serve money or wealth his spiritual eyes become dark and he cannot focus on and properly serve God. Many Christians attempt to serve God when they cannot even see Him, that is His will, because money and wealth have blinded them (cf. I Timothy 6:9-10).

In 6:25-34 Jesus naturally springs from a discussion of placing one's treasures in the right place, and not having divided allegiances to the issue of why it is ridiculous to be anxious. Jesus gives four major reasons why anxiety is ridiculous: 1) life is more than food and clothing (Mt. 6:25; cf. Lk. 12:13-21); 2) God is the One who is taking care of you (Mt. 6:26, 28-30); 3) you cannot accomplish anything by being anxious (6:27); and 4) when you are anxious you are demonstrating the attitude of an unsaved person (Mt. 6:31-32).

Hope

The Bible has much to say on the topic of hope. Someone has defined hope as "faith regarding the matters that are yet to be." This is a good definition of hope since Hebrews 11:1 says, "Now faith is the assurance of things hoped for, the convictions of things not seen." However, let us not be confused into thinking that hope is exhausted simply by a discussion of faith. Hope does have an identity of its own. *While faith is best viewed as the here and now reaching for the not yet, hope is best viewed as the not yet reaching into the now.* What we are going to see is that the not yet ought to affect the here and now.

Hope and Salvation

Hope is at the very foundation of our salvation. When the Bible speaks of hope, many times it is used as a synonym for salvation (Eph. 1:12; Heb. 6:18; 7:19; 10:23). This is significant because it tells us that hope can be understood in similar terms as salvation, in fact it can be used as a substitute term for it. Since hope is synonymous with salvation we know that there are both present and future benefits to hope. Also, it is a supernatural gift and not a man-based virtue. Further, it is centered in Christ. Plus, it cannot be lost or taken away. In addition, it is very important to the Christian life. All these are characteristics of salvation and therefore characteristics of hope.

Further, hope is that to which the believer is to be striving. The Bible is clear in its perspective towards the virtue of hope. Ephesians 1:18 and 4:4 tell us that the believer has been called to a specific hope. In other words, God had a purpose for which He called you. A purpose in the sense that He is going to do something with you. I Thessalonians 5:8 expands our understanding of what this purpose is. "But since we are of the day, let us be sober, having put on the breastplate of faith and love, and as a helmet, the hope of salvation." This verse indicates that the believer's hope is for salvation (the word "of" may be understood here to mean "for").

This is made clear by the following verse. "For God has not destined us for wrath, but for obtaining salvation through our Lord Jesus Christ" (5:9). "For" immediately tells us that Paul is about to explain his comments. He explains that God's destiny for us is not the wrath that the world will receive, but rather the obtaining or acquiring of the salvation that comes through Jesus Christ.

Sources of Hope

The Scriptures are quite clear on the sources of hope. There are clearly three to which it testifies: 1) Scripture itself–Romans 15:4; 2) the sequence of suffering, patience, and character–Romans 5:2-4; and 3) God Himself–Romans 15:13. Of particular interest in these three is the second one. In the hall of faith, which begins with Hebrews 11:1 and continues to the end of the chapter, you will note that while awaiting God's promises in faithful hope, each of the individuals mentioned endured suffering. In the midst of suffering they were patient because they knew the end, and their patience produced godly character. This indicates that Christians, who patiently suffer because of their hope, will find themselves growing in spiritual maturity.

Results of Hope

There are many outcomes of hope to which the Bible refers. Here, just a few will be noted, in order to determine how believers' lives ought to look, if they have really placed their hope where it truly ought to be.

Boldness: One of the first characteristics that hope produces is boldness. 2 Corinthians 3:12 clearly demonstrates that the reason Paul possessed so much boldness for the gospel was due to the fact that he had a right view of his hope. This should make believers thankful that God has supplied a glorious ministry of life for which they can receive power to testify regarding that life. Are we fully aware of exactly what God has done for us in salvation (read 2 Cor. 3:1-18 and Heb. 8-10)?

Identity: When the believer's life typifies his hope, he demonstrates himself to be a Christian. A life without hope is the life of an unsaved person. In both Ephesians 2:12 and 1 Thessalonians 5:8, Paul makes it very clear that a hopeless life is the type of life that an unsaved person leads. It is a life that has no hope in the future, but only this present life. Paul says that a life that is lived within the sphere of this world alone is a life to be pitied (1 Cor. 15:19).

Viewable: The believer's hope ought to be seen and noticed by others (1 Pet. 3:15). When people look at our lifestyle they ought to be asking how we can live in the manner that we do, in a positive sense. This means that our lives must be quantitatively different than the average man. If a Christian's life cannot be distinguished from the man on the street, he must ask himself if he is indeed different. Believers are under a mandate to grow. It is interesting to note that the exhortation in 1 Peter is given in the context of suffering for righteousness. (Take note of the earlier tie to suffering, patience, and character).

Purity: Finally, the ultimate result of our hope is purity. 1 John 3:3 says "And everyone who has this hope fixed on Him purifies himself, just as He is pure." What is this hope that John talks about? It is the hope of His final appearing, at which time we will be able to finally see Him, and that sight will reveal us to be like Him (cf. 2 Cor. 3:18). This is a fitting conclusion to this section, since it is where it started. In the introduction it was noted that hope is summed up as *the not yet* reaching into the *now*.

Love

One of the greatest discussions of the virtue of love found in all the world is that which is found in 1 Corinthians 13. Perhaps the most endearing verse regarding love in this chapter is 1 Corinthians 13:13, which says, "But now abide faith, hope, love, these three; but the greatest of these is love." This verse clearly indicates the priority of love over all other virtues. The thirteenth chapter of Corinthians falls in the midst of a rather lengthy discussion on the topic of spiritual matters, which spans from chapter twelve to chapter fourteen. It seems the Corinthian church was erroneously infatuated with the sign gifts.[1]

In chapter thirteen Paul argues that while the gifts are important and it is good to have and practice your gift, the greatest gift is love, and as such should be practiced by every believer. Chapter thirteen is the pivotal chapter in the section, showing what the focus of the gifts ought to be (in love for one another–14:1).

Paul begins 13:13 with the phrase "But now abide". Paul is drawing a contrast with this statement. What is the contrast that Paul is attempting to convey? There are two primary contrasts in this context: 1) a contrast of time (13:12); and 2) a contrast with the gifts (13:8). The virtues of faith surpass the exercise of gifts due to the nature of the gifts and the time of their practice. Gifts are temporary and gifts are for the purpose of producing Christian virtue, they are not an end in themselves (1 Cor. 12).

Paul then identifies the focus of the contrast as "faith, hope, and love, these three". It is interesting that all three of these elements is said to abide. But how is it possible that they will continue on into eternity? Someone accurately described the relationship between these three Christian virtues, when he said, "New objects of trust and desire will come into sight in the widening visions of the life eternal. Hope remains as the expectations of the ever-new unfolding of glory in the future state. Heaven is not one everlasting monotony which, when attained, leaves nothing further to expect. The angels sing ever-new praises to God. So we, too, shall pass from one to another of the joys which God has prepared for us. Faith and hope, as manifestations of love, will endure eternally." We may add to this statement that the finite mind can never, even in the eternal state, fully comprehend God. So learning of Him will be an eternal process.

Paul reminds his readers, however, that although all three abide, one is greater than the other two, "but the greatest of these is love." It is love because of its preeminence in character and traits. Unlike the other two, love is one of the characteristics of God, and it is what makes the Christian look like God (1 Cor. 8:3; 1 Jn. 4:7, 8, 12, 16). The Greeks possessed four terms for love, *storge* (love within family), *eros* (love motivated by passion), *philia* (love within friendships), and *agape* (rational love). Paul uses *agape* here, which was the highest form of love. It was a love that "called for recognition and judgment of value." It speaks to the esteem, admiration, and goodwill extended to another. It is a love that makes a decision regarding another to treat them in a certain way. In the New Testament this type of love is always concrete, that is, it is acting on the behalf of another (1 Cor. 13:1-8). This is not an emotional love that fluctuates with the ever ebbing and flowing of one's emotional or relational states. Rather, this love makes a decision of esteem regarding another and acts to that person according to that decision. One of the great expositions of this type of love is found in Philippians 4:1-4.

For the believer to grow as he ought, his life must be characterized by faith, hope, and love. All three are necessary while he walks here on the earth. Faith reaches out from where we are to the One whom we love, and hope focuses our minds on what will be in order to help us look more like the One we love. With these things in mind, we are now ready to begin looking at the issue of Christian beliefs and spiritual growth.

To give a historical perspective on each of the doctrinal areas affirmed throughout this book, as noted in the preface, an excerpt has been included as the opening statement of each chapter. These historical excerpts demonstrate the essential nature of that particular doctrinal area to the growth and life of the believer throughout church history.

Chapter Two
The Holy Scriptures

". . . 3. In proceeding to make mention of these things, I shall adopt, to commend my undertaking, the pattern of Luke the Evangelist, saying on my own account: 'Forasmuch as some have taken in hand,' to reduce into order for themselves the books termed apocryphal, and to mix them up with the divinely inspired Scripture, concerning which we have been fully persuaded, as they who from the beginning were eyewitnesses and ministers of the Word, delivered to the fathers; it seemed good to me also, having been urged thereto by true brethren, and having learned from the beginning, to set before you the books included in the Canon, and handed down, and accredited as Divine; to the end that any one who has fallen into error may condemn those who have led him astray; and that he who has continued steadfast in purity may again rejoice, having these things brought to his remembrance.
4. There are, then, of the Old Testament, twenty-two books in number; for, as I have heard, it is handed down that this is the number of the letters among the Hebrews; their respective order and

names being as follows. The first is Genesis, then Exodus, next Leviticus, after that Numbers, and then Deuteronomy. Following these there is Joshua, the son of Nun, then Judges, then Ruth. And again, after these four books of Kings, the first and second being reckoned as one book, and so likewise the third and fourth as one book. And again, the first and second of the Chronicles are reckoned as one book. Again Ezra, the first and second are similarly one book. After these there is the book of Psalms, then the Proverbs, next Ecclesiastes, and the Song of Songs. Job follows, then the Prophets, the twelve being reckoned as one book. Then Isaiah, one book, then Jeremiah with Baruch, Lamentations, and the epistle, one book; afterwards, Ezekiel and Daniel, each one book. Thus far constitutes the Old Testament.

5. Again it is not tedious to speak of the [books] of the New Testament. These are, the four Gospels, according to Matthew, Mark, Luke, and John. Afterwards, the Acts of the Apostles and Epistles (called Catholic), seven, viz. of James, one; of Peter, two; of John, three; after these, one of Jude. In addition, there are fourteen Epistles of Paul, written in this order. The first, to the Romans; then two to the Corinthians; after these, to the Galatians; next, to the Ephesians; then to the Philippians; then to the Colossians; after these, two to the Thessalonians, and that to the Hebrews; and again, two to Timothy; one to Titus; and lastly, that to Philemon. And besides, the Revelation of John.

6. These are fountains of salvation, that they who thirst may be satisfied with the living words they contain. In these alone is proclaimed the doctrine of godliness. Let no man add to these, neither let him take ought from these. For concerning these the Lord put to shame the Sadducees, and said, `Ye do err, not knowing the Scriptures.' And He reproved the Jews, saying, `Search the Scriptures, for these are they that testify of Me.'"[2]

No more important element of the Christian's walk is there than the Bible itself. It serves as the basis of how the Christian lives his life, and the manner in which he carries himself in the antagonistic world in which he lives. The Bible is in many ways a paradox. It is a book of great deep truths, while at the same time being a book of simple ideas that even a child can understand.

DOCTRINE

The first and foremost truth to understand, if one wants to possess a good understanding of the Bible, is the means by which God transferred the content of His Word from His mind to the books which became part of the Bible. The doctrinal truth that relates to this phenomena is the doctrine of special revelation. The Bible asserts that the act of special (having to do with the Bible) revelation (God communicating to man) is accomplished through God's interaction with mankind. These interactions were for the purpose of revealing God's will, works, and Himself (Ex. 3-13) to various men (2 Peter 1:20-21). The men who received this communication possessed varying skills and capabilities and God used different forms and modes of communication and interaction with each (Deut. 18:9-22; Dan. 8; John 15:26-27; 16:13; Book of Revelation). Revelation is also the resultant propositional content of that which He revealed by these acts, as they are recorded in the

Scripture, in other words, the Scriptures themselves (2 Timothy 3:16).

It was not just important to communicate the content of the Word to mankind, but God also had to assure that once communicated, it was actually accurate and reliable. This refers to the doctrine of inspiration. Inspiration is the act of God by which He, through the Holy Spirit, controlled the human authors of the Bible (2 Peter 1:20-21; 2 Timothy 3:16). This resulted in them being restrained from error (2 Timothy 3:16; John 16:13-15; 1 Cor. 2:1-13; Rom. 3:1-3; Tit. 1:2) as they were guided in their recording of His actual message (1 Pet. 1:10-12) and the actual historical events that illustrated and aided His message (Book Acts; 1 Cor. 15:1-11; Gal. 3). Inspiration applies specifically to the original writings (1 Tim. 5:18; 2 Pet. 3:16). They were guided in their individual abilities (evidenced when John's simple Greek is compared with the advanced Greek of Luke or Hebrews), situations (1 Corinthians answers questions; Luke is a history), memories (John 16:13-15), revelation (Num. 23), and sources (Luke 1:1-4; Old Testament quotes).

To this point it has been shown that God provided a means to communicate to us the content of His Word and to also verify that its content was actually reliable. The doctrine of illumination, next in line from revelation and inspiration, is very important in that it assures that the reliable Word can, in fact, be understood by man, the object of God's communication. It assures comprehension. Illumination is that work of the Holy Spirit whereby He unfolds both the meaning and application of the Word of God to the spiritually maturing believer (1 Cor. 2:1-16; 1 Jn. 2:18-27). This work enables him to understand without cloud or mystery and with full and absolute assurance the spiritual message of God in the spiritual words of God that have been recorded in the Bible (1 Cor. 2:13-16; 3:1-3; Heb. 5:11-14; 2 Cor 4:1-6; Col. 2:1-2).

    It is only natural that something so important to God for which He took the time to communicate its content, assure its reliability, and guarantee it could be understood, would also be important to His church. The Bible is the one source of information that affects the church's conduct. It provides the church with its rule of life and faith. It is from the Bible that God's people receive instruction on their conduct. The outcome of revelation, inspiration, and illumination, as they affect the Bible, is that the Word is the believer's only authoritative source for righteousness and conduct. The instruction found in its pages encourages the believer in his hope (Rom. 15:4). This same instruction also directs the believer away from craving evil things (1 Cor. 10:1-13). It is the only source needed for the believer's teaching, reproof, correction, and training in righteousness (2 Tim. 3:16). Because of this it fully provides him with all he needs for everything he will be called to do (2 Tim. 3:17). As such the believer is under a mandate to pay attention and take heed to this sure Word from God (2 Pet. 1:16-21).

APPLICATION

The Bible is in many ways the foundation of Spiritual Growth. Although the ultimate source and catalyst for spiritual growth is God, the means He uses most extensively is His Word. As such, the believer should have several responses to it: 1) Unhindered Allegiance; 2) Unwavering Obedience; and 3) Undiluted Pursuit.

Unhindered Allegiance

By unhindered allegiance it is meant that the Christian is to be committed to the truthfulness of the Word of God without question. The believer's response to the Bible is to be the same as his response to God, ". . . let God be found true, though every man be found a liar . . ."(Rom.3:4). Are you completely and absolutely committed to the truthfulness of Scripture, and to the fact that it is completely without error? In regard to the Christian's allegiance to the Word of God, 2 Timothy 4:1-4 has much to say. The immediate context of this passage focuses upon the last days, and their description as difficult times full of apostasy (leaving Christ) and false Christianity (2 Tim. 3:1-9). In response to this fact, Paul commends Timothy to remain true to both Paul's own teaching and lifestyle (3:10-13), as well as the teaching he received as a young man at the feet of his grandmother and mother (3:14-15). He concludes with a short discussion of the nature of Scripture and its accompanying results (3:16-17). Its nature, he indicates, is that it is the very Word of God. It is breathed out or inspired by God. Therefore, everything that the believer needs to live life springs from and comes from this inspired Word. As a response to both the direction of the world and the nature of the Scriptures themselves, Paul then in 4:1-2 charges Timothy to loyally proclaim the Word of God in every possible scenario. He then tells Timothy why in 4:3-4. The reasons are two-fold: 1) men in general will not endure sound doctrine, in other words they will not favor the things that the Bible teaches, but rather will turn away from the truth; and 2) men will amass for themselves people who will teach them what they want to hear, which will be based on their own desires, thus they will turn aside to myths. Why must a believer demonstrate unhindered allegiance to the Word of God? As the ultimate standard of truth, it outlines the only way the believer can live the life to which God has called him (cf. Jn. 6:66-71), and it is the very Word of God Himself. Therefore, we must cling to it. There are several principles that affect the believer's life based on this fact. They are:

1. The Bible stands as the one and only reliable source as to what it means to be a person.

2. The Bible can be clearly understood and comprehended without question and cloudiness.

3. The Bible does not compete with any man-made source that might attempt to compete with it for equal hearing.

4. The Bible holds Christians completely and absolutely responsible for their actions and behaviors in light of its teachings and principles.

5. The Bible is as much the spoken Word of God as the audible voice of God and is to be heeded in the same manner.[3]

In order for us to have and maintain this unhindered allegiance we must know without a shadow of a doubt that the Bible is the Word of God. If there are issues of mental assent, that is, areas with which you struggle regarding the divine nature of the Bible, then refer to appendix one. In this appendix, typical doubts regarding the Bible are answered in a general and informative manner.

Unwavering Obedience

By unwavering obedience it is meant that the Christian is to be committed completely to following whatever the Word of God says without question. The world, and sadly enough, the church has wandered far away from the biblical ideal, and as such the world, and sadly enough, many times the church finds the Bible's demands both difficult and foolish. The believer must therefore determine to live his life in full accord with the commands and dictates found in the Word. Believers cannot play with God's instructions. In Hebrews 12:29 after the author of Hebrews explained that New Testament believers have received a more powerful word than the Old Testament saints did, he reminds them that God is a "consuming fire." The implication is, if you don't play with fire, then you won't get burned. God should not be trifled with. In this section of Hebrews the author contrasts the word given at Sinai and the word given to the assembly, that is, the church (12:25-29). The word of Sinai (12:19-20), which is the Old Testament Law, came with physical manifestations of God's power and warning, causing fear and trembling (12:18, 20-21). The word, that is the one speaking (12:25) and voice (12:26), which comes to the assembly of God, the church, comes from the one called the Judge (12:23), the righteous man made perfect (12:23), Jesus, the mediator (12:24), situated in the heavenlies in the face of angels (12:22), and also comes with warnings (12:25). However, these warnings are even more binding than those of the old covenant, for these come from heaven rather than earth (12:25). Rather than resulting in the shaking of the earth, these are promised to shake both heaven and earth (12:26). In quoting Haggai 2:6 in 12:26 the author makes reference to the coming tribulation to precede the kingdom, the day spoken of in Hebrews 10:25, 37. Since believers belong to an unchangeable kingdom, they should rejoice in God with a recognition of the fact that God is a consuming fire. In other words, He is due the respect an obedient life illustrates. Therefore, one's belief about the Word must determine one's response to the Word. Do you struggle with some area of obedience? If there is some particularly difficult area with which you battle, please refer to appendix two for a topical presentation of common weaknesses and scriptural verses to memorize and meditate on in order to gain the victory. These can be used as a pattern for dealing with the other areas with which you may have problems that are not addressed here.

Undiluted Pursuit

Undiluted pursuit is the natural outcome of an unhindered allegiance and an unwavering obedience. If we stick tenaciously to the authority of the Bible and its truthfulness, and we consume ourselves with being obedient to it, then we must be committed to know the Word we stick tenaciously to and consume ourselves with. We must know God's Word. We get to know God's Word through several means: 1) we listen to the Word as it is faithfully preached at a Bible-believing, teaching, and preaching church (1 Tim. 4:6-16); 2) we study the Bible on our own in a systematic progressive way (Psa. 19:7-14); 3) we read it daily in a time of devotion with God (Psa. 1:2); 4) we meditate on its precepts and principles throughout the day (Psa. 1:2); and 5) we remain obedient to the light that we already have (Heb. 5:11-14). The most difficult struggles for the believer are those which center around points two and five. The development of obedience is the purpose for this writing. Therefore, we will not pause here to expound on it further. However, studying the Word is a very important aspect of the believer's life. For your assistance, included in appendix three is a simple method of approaching your personal study and devotional time.

Chapter Three
The Godhead

"In the course of time, then, the Father forsooth was born, and the Father suffered, – God Himself, the Lord Almighty, whom in their preaching they declare to be Jesus Christ. We, however, as we indeed always have done (and more especially since we have been better instructed by the Paraclete, who leads men indeed into all truth), believe that there is one only God, but under the following dispensation, or oikonomia, as it is called, that this one only God has also a Son, His Word, who proceeded from Himself, by whom all things were made, and without whom nothing was made. Him we believe to have been sent by the Father into the Virgin, and to have been born of her – being both Man and God, the Son of Man and the Son of God, and to have been called by the name of Jesus Christ; we believe Him to have suffered, died, and been buried, according to the Scriptures, and, after He had been raised again by the Father and taken back to heaven, to be sitting at the right hand of the Father, and that He will come to judge the quick and the dead; who sent also from heaven from the Father, according to His own promise, the Holy Ghost, the Paraclete, the sanctifier of the faith of those who believe in the Father, and in the Son, and in the Holy Ghost. That

this rule of faith has come down to us from the beginning of the gospel, even before any of the older heretics, much more before Praxeas, a pretender of yesterday, will be apparent both from the lateness of date which marks all heresies, and also from the absolutely novel character of our new-fangled Praxeas. In this principle also we must henceforth find a presumption of equal force against all heresies whatsoever – that whatever is first is true, whereas that is spurious which is later in date. But keeping this prescriptive rule inviolate, still some opportunity must be given for reviewing (the statements of heretics), with a view to the instruction and protection of diverse persons; were it only that it may not seem that each perversion of the truth is condemned without examination, and simply prejudged; especially in the case of this heresy, in thinking that one cannot believe in One Only God in any other way than by saying that the Father, the Son, and the Holy Ghost are the very selfsame Person. As if in this way also one were not All, in that All are of One, by unity (that is) of substance; while the mystery of the dispensation is still guarded, which distributes the Unity into a Trinity, placing in their order the three Persons – the Father, the Son, and the Holy Ghost: three, however, not in condition, but in degree; not in substance, but in form; not in power, but in aspect; yet of one substance, and of one condition, and of one power, inasmuch as He is one God, from whom these degrees and forms and aspects are reckoned, under the name of the Father, and of the Son, and of the Holy Ghost. How they are susceptible of number without division, will be shown as our treatise proceeds."[4]

DOCTRINE

The Nature of the Trinity

The truth of the doctrine of the Trinity simply put is that God exists in a state that is best described as three persons in one essence. When we say one essence we mean that each of the Trinitarian persons possesses all of the divine nature (Father-100%; Son-100%; Spirit-100%) in such a way that there can only properly exist one God (Jn. 1:1-18; 10:30; 20:28; Phil. 2:6; Col. 2:9; Heb. 1:10-12; Act. 5:3-4). Unlike individual humans who possess only part of the entire human nature, being able to produce other human beings who share in their human nature, the divine nature cannot be shared or replicated. This one divine being exists in three persons. Each individual of the Trinity is distinct, yet they are in such a unity that they are in fact one in being/essence.

When discussing the Trinity we must make two distinctions regarding the Godhead's functions or operations. They are: 1) the internal elements of the Trinity–the interrelationship of the members of the Trinity; and 2) the external elements of the Trinity–relationship of the members of the Trinity to creation.

The internal elements of the Trinity deals with works within the Trinity, that is, how each member relates to the other members. In discussing the internal relationships of the Trinity, the Father sends (Jn. 14:16-17, 26), the Son is both sent and sends (Jn. 15:26; 16:7), and the Holy Spirit is sent (Jn. 14:16-17, 26). The Father begets the Son, while the Son is begotten but not proceeding; the Holy Spirit, who does not beget, proceeds from the Father and the Son.[5]

The external elements of the Trinity deal with works outside of the Godhead. In discussing the external relationship of the Trinity, the order of activity is **of** the Father, **through** the Son, **by** the Holy Spirit, **unto** the Father. In other words, the Father is positioned in Scripture as the originator of all things and all actions the Godhead does. The Son is described as the medium through whom the Godhead's, particularly the Father's, plans are worked and carried out. The Holy Spirit is identified as the agent that carries out what the Son is to execute. In this regard, the Father elects (1 Pet. 1:1-2), loves (Jn. 3:16), and gives (Jam. 1:17); the Son suffers (Mk. 8:31), redeems (1 Pet. 1:18-19), and upholds (Heb. 1:3); and the Holy Spirit regenerates (Ti. 3:5), energizes (Eph. 1:13-14; Ac. 1:8) and sanctifies (Gal. 5:22, 23).

The Attributes of the Trinity

There are several ways that Christians have classified God's attributes, each of which has its negatives and positives. For the purposes of this brief discussion we will break them down into communicable and incommunicable attributes.

By communicable, we mean those attributes that God possesses which have some analogy in human beings. The communicable attributes would be *omniscience*—God knows all things (Psalm 139:16; 147:4; Mt. 10:29-30); *omnipotence*—God is all powerful (Gen. 17:1; Ex. 6:3; Ps.

91:1; Jer. 32:17; Mt. 19:26; Lk. 1:37; 2 Cor. 6:18; Rev. 1:8); *wisdom*—God does the best things possible (Job 9:3-4; Prov. 1:20-33; Dan. 2:20, 23; Matt. 11:26; Rom. 11:33-36); *holiness*—God is perfectly free of any defilement (Ex. 15:11; Lev. 19:2; 1 Sam. 2:2; Ps. 5:4; 47:8; Is. 6:3; 57:15; Ezek. 39:7; Hab. 1:13; Rev. 4:8); *justice/righteousness*—God does only what is right (Gen. 18:25; Ezra 9:15; Ps. 11:7; 33:4-5; 89:14; 119:137; Isa. 3:10-11; Rom. 3:25-26; 2 Thess. 1:3-10); *love*—God is committed to His people (Jn. 3:16; Rom. 5:8; 1 Jn. 4:8); *goodness*—God shows mercy and grace to His people (Isa. 54:7; Rom. 9:15, 18; Eph. 2:4-5); *truth/veracity*—God is completely reliable as to His Word, nature, and conduct (Num. 23:19; Ps. 19:9; 89:14; 111:8; Jn. 14:6; 17:3; Rom. 3:4); *will of God/freedom*—God is completely uncoerced in what He does, He does whatever He pleases (Isa. 40:13; Matt. 11:26).

By incommunicable, we mean those attributes that God possesses which have no analogy in human beings. The incommunicable attributes are *self-existence*—God is uncaused as to His being or existence (Ex. 3:14; Isa. 43:10; 44:6; Jn. 5:26; Ac. 17:24; Rom. 11:36); *simplicity*—God is not susceptible to procession in time, thought, etc. (Deut. 6:4; Isa. 44:6; 1 Cor. 8:4); *unity*—God exists in perfect harmony (Same as above); *infinite*—God is beyond time and space (1 Kin. 8:27; Ps. 90:2; Acts 17:24-28); *eternity*—God has always existed and is not bound by time (Ps. 102:24-27; Is. 46:9-10); *immutability*—God does not change (Num. 23:19; 1 Sam. 15:29; Is. 46:9-10); *omnipresence*—Everything is in God's presence (Ps. 139:7-12); *immensity*—God is beyond space boundaries (Ps.

139:7-12; Job. 11:7-9; Isa. 66:1); and *sovereignty*—God controls all things (Ps. 47:8; 135:6; Acts 15:18; Eph. 1:11).

The Decrees of God

The decrees of God refer to the individual purposes of God, which when logically and temporally placed into one unifying plan, we refer to as the decree of God. The divine decree is the theological label which is associated with the fulfillment of God's plan or God's sovereign ordering of His universe. By God's divine decree we mean that eternal (Psa. 33:11; Ac. 15:18; Eph. 1:11; 2 Tim. 1:9) plan of God (Rom. 8:28; Eph. 1:11; 3:11) whereby, based on His inscrutable wisdom, holiness, and goodness, He freely and without any basis outside of Himself sets for certain what will come to pass in the universe (Isa. 14:26-27; 46:10-11; Dan. 4:35; Eph. 1:11).

An example of the decrees are as follows: 1) creation; 2) the fall; 3) election; and 4) provision for salvation. The decrees are divided into the efficacious decrees and permissive decrees. The efficacious decrees are those actively brought about by God. The permissive decrees are those decrees that are passively allowed by God to occur. This type of decree deals only with evil. While the event is set as certain, it is done so without the immediate action of God Himself, so God does not enable men and angels to sin against Himself.

APPLICATION

God, specifically the Son, is the object of our faith. Faith plays an intricate role in the life of the believer. It is through faith that the believer finds God and has access to Him. It can be simply put, that without faith it is impossible to please God (Hebrews 11:6). Faith reaches out to the Unseen God and makes His works and power felt in the world of the seen. Faith is that by which the believer touches the untouchable, and understands the incomprehensible. Faith is an intricate aspect of the believer's walk. There are several important things that the believer should know and understand about faith in order to enable him to live a more faithful life. Faith is 1) grounded; 2) comprehensive; and 3) progressive. These elements will be explained below.

Faith is Grounded

The fact that faith is grounded manifests itself throughout Scripture. By grounded, it is meant that it is not a blind leap. Some have misunderstood the opening verse of Hebrews eleven, which says, "Now faith is the assurance of things hoped for, the conviction of things not seen," to mean that faith is a blind leap, an uniformed quest or journey. However, such an interpretation, while it is understandable, cannot be substantiated from the text of Hebrews eleven. One only needs to read through the rest of the chapter to see that faith is always based on something, which is always the person or word of God.

Each of the examples that are given in chapter eleven are invoked because of their simple and immediate obedience to the word of God. While the outcome of their faith may not have been seen or known (11:13, 39-40), the object of their faith was clearly known and understood. It was the word or promise of God (11:13, 39-40). Faith took the object of their faith, and enabled them to act as if the outcome of their faith was actualized.

Let us look at just one example. The example of Noah is clear and precise. Noah is the third person mentioned in the Hall of Faith. The author prefaces his comments about Noah with "by faith". So, what follows springs from his faith. The word of God as represented in this passage is "being warned by God about things not yet seen . . ." This is in reference to the fact of rain and flood, which apparently had not happened since there is no indication that the world's condition had changed from Genesis 2:4-6. Thus, Noah had no more than the word of God indicating that there was going to be a devastating flood, which was something unseen to him, and for that fact, unknown. The response of Noah to this information is immediate obedience. God had also communicated to him in His word what his response to this event was to be, he was to build a boat (Gen. 6:14-20). This he did, according to the author of Hebrews in that he "prepared an ark" (Heb. 11:7; cf. Gen. 6:21-22). The attitude in which he did it is described as "in reverence". In reverence to what? To God and His word. The outcome of his decision is that his family was saved, the world was properly judged, and he became an heir of righteousness (Heb. 11:7).

The principles are clear from this example. Faith is grounded in or on the Word and person of God. When faith is grounded it responds to the Word and person of God with reverent and immediate obedience. Such acts of faith result in God's desired outcome. Every believer has different situations or hindrances that present problems to them in their Christian walk. For a list of specific hindrances and matching biblical passages to help overcome them, refer to appendix four.

Faith is Comprehensive

By describing faith as comprehensive, it is meant that faith encompasses all of mankind's being. No part of him is left out of the process. A simple, practical way to remember the implications of this aspect to faith, is that it involves the mind, the heart, the hands, and the feet. Faith involves the mind, in that it causes the person possessing faith to think differently. Faith leads a person to think in different categories than the unsaved. Rather than thinking that the visible is the only real world, the believer knows that the visible is oftentimes simply a reflection of the invisible. This causes him to realize that there is a whole unseen world with which he has to interact (2 Cor. 10:1-6). Faith propels the believer to think that God is able to do those things which the world says are impossible or cannot happen (cf. Rom. 4:16-21; and Heb. 11:19–notice the mental terms like contemplated and considered). Faith affects your thinking.

Faith also affects your heart. It is from your heart that your motives and your will are produced (Gen. 6:5; 8:21; Mt. 12:33-37; 15:15-20). It is also from a person's heart that belief or faith springs (Rom. 10:9-10). As such, faith takes what the mind perceives and puts it into action through the will.

Faith also affects the hands, or what we do. Faith makes the believer behave differently than the world around him. The words of James are very clear when he says, "What use is it, my brethren, if a man says he has faith, but he has no works? Can that faith save him? If a brother or sister is without clothing and in need of daily food, and one of you says to them, 'Go in peace, be warmed and be filled,' and yet you do not give them what is necessary for their body, what use is that? Even so faith, if it has no works, is dead, being by itself" (James 2:14-17). Faith affects our hands. It urges us to work for our Lord, rather than for man.

Finally, faith affects our feet, or where we go. Faith makes us join with the household of faith, not putting it off as unimportant, but being faithful (cf. Heb. 10:23-25). Faith makes us go where God says to go even if we cannot see where it will lead (Heb. 11:8), or even if we are being enticed to go where we should not (11:24-27; cf. 1 Pet.4:4).

Faith is Progressive

The progressive nature of faith relates to the fact that faith and the practice thereof is a growth process. Since one's faith is so intricately tied to one's knowledge and relationship to God, then as one grows in that relationship, his faith in turn deepens or becomes richer. The issue of faith is, what do you believe God is able to do? This will oftentimes be answered differently by a baby Christian and a more mature Christian. The latter has a fuller appreciation of the One to whom he is related and thus can believe Him to an even greater extent. One's level of spiritual maturity has a lot to do with the choices and decisions that they make (1 Cor. 2:14-16).

Not only is faith progressive in the sense of progressing in relationship, but also it is progressive in the sense of beginning the Christian life, continuing the Christian life, and the consummation of the Christian life. In Romans 1:17 Paul says that the righteousness of God is made known "from faith to faith." In this phrase he means that the Christian life starts with faith (justification), continues with faith (sanctification), and is consummated by faith (glorification) (cf. 8:30).[6] The Christian life can only be lived by faith. Paul warns the Galatians that having begun by faith, it is impossible to be perfected by works (3:1-5). This is the common trap of legalism and is discussed in appendix four.

Part Two

♦

God's Handiwork

The Creation of Angels and Man
and Their Implication for Spiritual Growth

Chapter Four
THE EXISTENCE AND ROLE OF ANGELIC BEINGS

After arguing that Christ possessed a soul and in some way, unknown to us men, God must possess a soul as well, although He is simple (that is, He cannot be divided into parts), the church father Origen makes the following statement regarding angels: *"And therefore there seems to me no absurdity in either understanding or asserting some such thing regarding the holy angels and the other heavenly powers, since that definition of soul appears applicable also to them. For who can rationally deny that they are "sensible and moveable?" But if that definition appears to be correct, according to which a soul is said to be a substance rationally "sensible and moveable," the same definition would seems also to apply to angels. For what else is in them than rational feeling and motion? Now those beings who are comprehended under the same definition have undoubtedly the same substance."*[7]

DOCTRINE

The Nature of Angels (Elect and Evil)

Angels, both elect and evil, are created beings as is man (Gen. 1:1; Job 38:4-7). They are part of the creation sequence in Genesis 1. They were created through the actions of Christ (Jn. 1:1-3; Col. 1:16). They seem to have been created *ex nihilo*, which means *out of nothing* (Col. 1:16), through the direct command of God. They were created in holiness, specifically that they might glorify God (Ps. 148:2; Rev. 4:6-11).

Angelic beings, both elect and evil, are considered to be persons. One definition of personhood is the possession of intellect, emotions, will, and dominion. Angels possess all four of these characteristics. First, intellect, the ability to reason, is witnessed to by the fact that they can communicate in speech (Is. 6:1-4; 1 Pet. 1:12; Mt. 28:5). Their possession of emotions, the ability to feel, is also evidenced in Scripture (Job. 38:7; Lk. 15:10). That angels have the ability to choose freely amongst options evidences their possession of a will (Is. 14:12-15; Lk. 8:28-31). The fourth characteristic that testifies to angels being persons is the possession of dominion, the ability and power to rule or exhibit authority. This is testified to by use of the following terms to describe them: rulers or principalities (Rom. 8:38; Eph. 3:10; 6:12; Col. 1:16; 2:15), authorities and powers (Eph. 1:21; 2:2; 3:10; 6:12; Col. 1:16; 2:15; 1 Pet. 3:22), and thrones or dominions (Col. 1:16). All of these terms have to do with the possession and exercise of power and authority, and all are exhibited in angels.

The existence of demons (evil angels) is affirmed in both the Old Testament and the New Testament. If it were possible for Satan to fall, who was the highest created angelic being, then the possibility of lesser angelic beings falling is not surprising. It may be implied that since the highest one fell, he may very well have taken others with him. While Satan's angels are never referred to as Satan's demons, it may be assumed, since the Bible indicates that he does have his own angels, that these are what the Bible refers to as demons (Matt. 25:41; Rev. 12:9).

While the Old Testament mentions demons (Lev. 17:7; Deut. 32:17; Ps. 106:37), it is the New Testament that is clearer as to their existence. Our Lord and all the New Testament writers mention demons, except the author of Hebrews. Jesus affirms their existence, in that He talked to and cast out what He stated to be demons (Matt. 12:22-29; 15:22-28; 17:14-20; 25:41; Mk. 5:1-16; Lk. 10:17-18). Further, Paul (1 Corinthians 10:20-21), James (James 2:19), and John (Revelation 9:20) have specific teaching on the existence of demons.

The Divisions of Angels

The Bible has more indirect teaching than direct teaching about the various kinds and ranks of angels. However, we can make some conclusions about the kinds of angelic beings in existence. They are the Archangels, Cherubim, and Seraphim.

There is only one angel referred to as the Archangel, and that is Michael (Dan. 10:13, 21; 12:1; Jude 9). This may be a special designation that sets him apart among the highest ranking angels. He seems to have a special authority with three special duties. He is endowed with the authority of God (Dan. 10:13; Rev. 12:7-10), and stands for God's people Israel (Dan. 10:21; 12:1), as well as opposes God's enemies (Dan. 10:13; Jude 9; Rev. 12:7-10).

The Cherubim are the highest class of angels, having as their duty the guarding, protecting, and proclaiming of God's holiness, glorious presence, and sovereignty (Gen. 3:24; Ex. 25:10-22; 36:8ff; 1 Kgs. 6:23-29; Eze. 10:15-20; 28:14, 16; 41:18-20).

The next rank of angels seems to be the Seraphim, having as their duty the exposition (proclamation) of God's holiness and ethical loftiness. They are called burning ones, which gives an accurate picture of the intensity of their devotion to God's holiness (Is. 6:2, 6).

The Roles of Angels (Elect and Evil)

Angelic activity is very pervasive throughout the Bible. While they are involved in governmental realms of activity in the universe according to Daniel (Dan. 10-11), they are not just limited to that global aspect. From the Biblical text it is evident that both Elect and Evil Angels are very active. The activity of

Elect Angels may be divided into five areas including angelic relationships to: 1) God; 2) Christ; 3) the world; 4) unbelievers; and 5) believers. The activity of Evil Angels may be divided into their demonic activity with reference to: 1) God; 2) unbelievers; and 3) believers.

ELECT ANGELS. Key Word(s): *Service and Assistance.* As to their relationship to God, they praise Him (Psa. 103:20; 148:1-2; Isa. 6:3), worship Him (Isa. 6:3; Heb. 1:6; Rev. 5:8-13), rejoice in His acts (Job 38:6-7), serve His ends (Rev. 7:1; 22:9), are accountable to Him (Job. 1:6; 2:1), and aid the outworking of His plan (Rev. 7:1; 8:2). Key Word(s): *Service and Assistance.* To Christ, they predicted and announced His birth (Mt. 1:20; Lk. 1:26-28; 2:8-15), watched out for and carried out His protection (Mt. 2:13-15, 19-21), ministered to His needs (Mt. 4:6, 11; 26:53; Lk. 22:43), aided and announced His resurrection and ascension (Mt. 28:1-2, 5-6; Lk. 24:4-7; Ac. 1:10-11), and will aid and participate in His rapturing of the church and His second coming (Mt. 13:39-40; 25:31; 1 Thess. 4:16; 2 Thess. 1:7). Key Word(s): *Influence.* As to the world, they watch over and influence national leaders (Dan. 4:17; 10:21; 11:1; 12:1; Rev. 8-9, 16). Key Word(s): *Inflict.* In reference to unbelievers, they announce, inflict, and carry out judgment on them (Gen. 19:13; Mt. 13:39-40; Ac. 12:23; Rev. 14:6-7; 16:1; 19:17-18). Key Word(s): *Minister to and Protection of.* In their relationship to believers, they helped believers in communicating and revealing some of the truth that became part of the Bible (Dan. 7:15-27; 8:13-26; Rev. 1:1; 22:6, 8), bring answers to prayer (Dan. 9:20-27 Ac. 12:5-10), assist in saving people (Ac. 8:26; 10:3), watch the events in the church (1 Cor. 4:9; 11:10; Eph. 3:10; 1 Tim. 5:21; 1 Pet. 1:12), exhort in times of danger (Ac. 27:23-24), and watch over and care for the righteous even at the time of death (Lk. 16:22; Ac. 12:5-10; Heb. 1:14).

EVIL ANGELS. Much of the information regarding the work of the demons comes from the work of their leader. Key Word(s): *Resist*. As to their relationship to God, they promote rebellion (as does Satan–Gen. 3; 2 The. 2:3-4), slander (as Satan does, so do his angels–Gen. 3:1-5; Job 1:9; Zec. 3:1; Rev. 12:10), idolatry (Lev. 17:7; Deut. 32:17; 2 Chron. 11:15; Ps. 106:37; 1 Cor. 10:20; 12:2), and they reject grace (2 Cor. 4:3-4; 1 Ti. 4:1-8). Key Word(s): *Afflict*. They afflict mankind with physical diseases (Mt. 9:33; 12:22; Lk. 13:11-17). Not all physical and mental disorders are caused by demons, even the Bible distinguishes between the two (Mt. 4:24; Mk. 1:32; Lk. 7:21; 9:1; Jn. 9:1-12). They possess unbelievers (see above references), and may hinder believers (see following passages). Key Word(s): *Resist and Hinder*. Demons oppose believers, causing them to have to struggle against them in the armor of God, and not their own strength (Eph. 6:10-12). They attempt to influence and direct individual Christians (Acts 5:1-11). They also oppose the church in general, promoting false doctrine (1 Tim. 4:1-3), libertinism (2 Peter. 2:1-4), and divisions (Jam. 3:14-16). They also counter the gospel ministry

(2 Cor. 4:3-4), and pervert the gospel (2 Cor. 11:13-15), as well as promote persecution (Rev. 2:8-10).

The Nature and Activity of Satan

Any justified reading of the text of Scripture leaves little doubt as to the existence of Satan. The Biblical teaching of Scripture is usually organized around three hubs: 1) his reality; 2) his original state and fall; and 3) his present state and activity.

As to his reality, it is clear that he is a person or literally exists since he evidences intellect, emotions, will, and dominion (as defined above), as well as being referred to with personal pronouns, and being held morally responsible for his acts (Job. 1-2; Mt. 4:1-11; 12:22-29; Jn. 12:31).

Satan's original state was one of glory and honor. In this state he was of the Cherub class of angels, and was probably the leader amongst that class, because the Bible indicates that he was unparalleled amongst the created beings in perfection and wisdom. He was the chief guardian of God's holiness, majesty, and presence, abiding in the very presence of God Himself. He had total moral integrity. In this state he was the zenith or epic of God's creation, having an unparalleled position in God's universe (Is. 14:12-14; Eze. 28:11-19).

The immediate cause of Satan's fall was a case of a proud heart and self-occupation. He became enthralled with himself and as a result was indicted by God and cast out of heaven. His character was corrupted, his power perverted, and his destiny was set to be the pit (Is. 14:12-14; Eze. 28:11-19; Mt. 25:41; 1 Tim. 3:6). The time of his fall was sometime before the events of Genesis 3, and after the events of Genesis 2.

The Bible now depicts Satan as an adversary, an opposer of God, His people, and His acts (Jude 9; Rev. 12:9; 20:2), a slanderer (Rev. 12:9; 20:2), the epitome of evil (Jn. 17:15; 2 Cor. 6:15; 1 Jn. 5:18-19), ferocious in battle (1 Pet. 5:8; Rev. 12:3-17), the accuser of believers (Zech. 3:1-5; Rev. 12:9-10), the tempter (1 Chron. 21:1; Lk. 22:31; Ac. 5:3; 1 Cor. 7:5; 2 Cor. 11:3; 1 Thess. 3:5), a murderer and a liar (Jn. 8:44), and an entrapper (2 Tim. 2:26). He is the ruler of this world system (Jn. 12:31; 16:11; Eph. 2:2), god of this world (2 Cor. 4:4), ruler of fallen angels (Rev. 12:7-9), and controller and father of unbelievers (Jn. 8:44).

APPLICATION

The believer finds himself encompassed about by a whole unseen world with which he must have interaction. There is no option for the believer. Whether he likes it or not, he is involved in the unseen activities of the universe. When he prays, unseen messengers relay his request to God. When he is in danger, unseen guardians protect him from harm. However, when he is in conflict, such conflict although it looks physical, is in actuality spiritual. It is a battle in which the weapons of this world will not satisfy. There are many important aspects to spiritual growth that relate to the spiritual powers found in the universe, but we will focus on just three. Because of the Spiritual Powers (good and evil) involved in the believer's life, he must: 1) Engage the Right Battle; 2) Outfit the Right Armor; and 3) Maintain the Right Focus. Each of these plays an important role in our spiritual growth.

Engage the Right Battle

In speaking of the believer's battle, we begin with the believer's need to "Engage the Right Battle," because if he is not sure of the battle that he is in, he will not know the right armor to put on or the right focus to keep. As such, we must first determine the nature of the battle. There is no better passage of Scripture that defines the believer's battle than that found in Ephesians 6:10-13. In this passage Paul clearly lays out the nature of the battle by a clear call for the believer to outfit himself in the entire armor of God (6:10-13). The purpose is to enable the believer to stand in the battle (6:13). In these four verses, Paul gives three defining characteristics of the battle or war in which the believer is engaged. First, Paul refers to it as standing "firm against the schemes of the devil." "Schemes" is taken from the Greek word from which the English word "method" is derived. It is the idea of that which pursues an "orderly and technical procedure in the handling of something." So the battle is something in which the devil has mapped out what he wants to accomplish. He has a particular *modus operandi*, that is, a way by which he operates. He is plotting and planning how he will approach your particular foothold in the war.

Second, Paul refers to the battle as a "struggle." This word was used in reference to a wrestling match, a hand to hand fight. In such combats all manner of techniques were used in order to bring the opponent under submission, whether it be trickery, cunning, or strategy. The opponents did whatever it took to win the battle. We fight an enemy who is willing to use whatever means at his disposal in order to overcome us. We must be prepared to withstand his onslaughts through the armor of God.

Third, Paul tells the believers at Ephesus that they must "resist in the evil day." To "resist" means to stand against, withstand, or oppose. The battle is one in which the believer must set himself squarely against his foe. He cannot half-heartedly approach his enemy, but rather he must face his foe with the goal of resisting him and turning him back. This idea is emphasized by Paul's parallel idea of "stand firm," which appears at the end of the verse.

So the believer finds himself in a battle in which he is squared off against Satan, who is using all of his tricks, strategies, and skills in order to overcome him and make him a useless warrior for his King. How can a believer possibly fight in such a battle? Paul points his readers to the right armor for the battle.

Outfit the Right Armor

Because the believer does find himself in a battle, he must be sure that he outfits himself with the right armor to face it. Just as a soldier without his armor is open prey for the enemy, so it is with the Christian who is without his proper protective gear. Armor does not just defend, armor also frees the soldier up to fight even more vigorously. Once he feels secure in his defense, he can then throw his mind into the battle wholeheartedly. Once the believer is secure in his armor, he can feel free to more exuberantly engage the enemy in war. What is to be the believer's armor? Paul identifies and explains the believer's armor in Ephesians 6:14-19. In trying to understand this passage, many have focused upon the parts of the armor to the neglect of the virtues that the armor represents. This is not Paul's point. Paul is emphasizing and focusing upon the virtues themselves as the believer's armor. Each point stated about each virtue is a summary of an element of his preceding teaching in the book of Ephesians.

Truth: The first virtue that Paul puts forth is that of truth. In general, truth is that which refers or corresponds to reality. In other words, how something corresponds to what actually is. In Ephesians, truth has three nuances related to that meaning. It can be seen: 1) as another term for the gospel (1:13); 2) as a state of being or position (4:21, 24; 5:9); and 3) as a practical expression of one's character (4:15, 25). The importance of truth to the battle in which the Christian is involved is related to the fact that the believer's enemy deals in falsehood (2 Cor.

11:14; 1 Tim. 4:1-5; Rev. 12:9). It is no surprise that Paul begins this list with truth, because it is always the position of Scripture that truth comes before all else. This is why James said that the wisdom of God, is first pure, as to its truthfulness, before it is anything else (James 3:17). The only way to counteract Satan's lies is to know and live by the truth (Jn. 8:31-32, 44).

Righteousness: The second virtue mentioned in this passage is righteousness. Righteous refers to conformity to all that God commands, appoints, or claims. Righteousness may be either positional or practical. Positionally, it means a state of right standing before God, being properly related to him (Eph. 4:24). It also has practical ramifications, however. In 5:8 Paul commends the Ephesians to walk in the light. Such walking is characterized by righteousness. The focus of the enemy is to make the believer stray from the commands or directions of the Lord. This is his function as the tempter (1 Cor. 7:5; 2 Cor. 11:3; 1 Thess. 3:5). Satan is also the accuser of the brethren (Rev. 12:10) and as such, one of the best defenses the believer has against his insidious attacks is a life of righteousness. Rather than being carried away by temptation and choosing the enemy's way or being justly accused by his snaring accusations, the believer needs to outfit himself in the righteousness of the Lord both positionally and practically.

Gospel: The next virtue that Paul makes mention of is the gospel of peace. Paul speaks of the gospel three other times in this epistle. In 1:13 it is called the "message of truth" which brought salvation and sealing of the Holy Spirit. 3:6 speaks of the gospel as that which has brought the Jews and Gentiles together, establishing peace (cf. 2:11-22). This gospel, Paul asserts, is a mystery revealed (6:19; cf. 3:4; 5:32). The peace of the gospel is very important for the believer when he is in combat. First, the peace between fellow soldiers is important since a dis-unified army is a destroyed army (cf. Lk. 11:17). Second, the peace of the warrior himself is important if he is going to fight unhindered. A soldier unsure of the reason or purpose of the battle is a defeated soldier. He must be infected with the very thing for which he is fighting. In spiritual terms, Satan tries to unbalance the soldier by making him doubt his position and standing with God, and it is only through the gospel which produces peace that he can truly have peace in the midst of the battle.

Faith: The fourth virtue that Paul commends to the Ephesians' ears is that of the shield of faith. Faith, always an extensive subject in Paul's writings, occupies an important part in this epistle as well. Faith refers to the complete or confident trust in Christ, as well as the "constant openness to (and appropriation of) God's resources in Christ." It may speak of the practical elements of belief and appropriation, or the things believed themselves. Both the former (1:15; 2:8; 3:12, 17; 6:23) and the latter (4:5; 13) meanings are found in the book of Ephesians. The shield of faith is the only part of the believer's armor that comes with an explanation of its usage. Paul says that faith enables the believer "to extinguish" Satan's "flaming missiles." It is through faith that the believer is able to render powerless Satan's multiplicity of exploding missiles like doubt, lust, greed, envy, hate, bitterness, tribulation, etc., as well as receive confidence in his battle with the evil one.

Salvation: Paul then moves on to the soldier's helmet, which he calls salvation. As used in the other references to salvation in Ephesians, salvation means that the believer has been rescued or delivered from the realm of Satan, to the realm of Christ (1:13; 2:5, 8). In the midst of this spiritual battle, the believer must have full assurance both of his present position in Christ, as well as his future hope in Christ. Satan will attempt to remove him from this confidence or assurance if at all possible. His ploy is to assail him both externally (trying to create barriers and blocks) as well as internally (trying to create doubt and confusion). When the external attacks begin to distract the believer, he must remember that he has been rescued out of the land of the evil one and no longer has to live according to that manner of life (Eph. 2:1-10; 4:17-5:21; cf. Jn. 16:31-33 with 1 Jn. 4:4). When the internal distractions come his way he must focus his attention on the Word of God and the promise that it holds for him.[8]

Word of God: The last virtue that Paul places in the armor is that of the "sword of the Spirit." Paul defines the sword not as to its function, but as to its nature. It is the Word of God. His only other use of the Word in this epistle is found in 5:26, where the Word is said to be that which Christ uses to sanctify the church through cleansing it. The Word of God is critical in the Christian's battle. It has the distinct function of being both an offensive and a defensive weapon. No other piece of the armor has this distinction. This dual nature of the Word of God is most clearly seen in the temptation of Christ by Satan himself (Mt. 4:1-11). During His temptation, Christ not only blocks Satan's attack, but He also sends a strong thrust at the adversary himself. If we desire to properly engage in the battle, we must know and effectively use the Word of God.

Maintain the Right Focus

When one is in the midst of a battle, war, or conflict, one of the greatest dangers that presents itself to him is the danger of distractions. A distraction causes the person to lose focus. This is particularly dangerous to the believer in his spiritual battle, because once your focus is displaced, the battle is then in favor of the opponent. It is imperative that he "Maintain the Right Focus." The apostle Paul consistently found himself in the midst of spiritual warfare. Paul was a Spiritual Green Beret, and as such we ought to listen to him when he talks about spiritual warfare.

The book of 2 Corinthians was written during a time in Paul's ministry when he was under great attack and assault. Because the war of the believer is essentially a spiritual one, coupled with the fact that we are humans, it is easy for us to lose sight of the spiritual nature of the battle. When that occurs, we focus on the physical elements of our existence or battle. These elements may be relationships, tribulations, or temptations that lure our eyes from the spiritual. Paul was at this time experiencing all three: 1) relationships–the Corinthian church was improving but still had much growth ahead of them; 2) tribulations–his apostleship, and his very integrity were being called into question by his enemies and some in the Corinthian church; and 3) temptations–he was struggling with whether he should be soft with them, when he really needed to be very firm.

In the midst of this, however, Paul writes 2 Corinthians 10:1-6 indicating the position of his focus. Paul states in 10:1-2 that there were some who thought him to be merely a man, and that his power and authority were only that of any other man. Paul's response was, though he exists in the physical world, he does not fight the battle of that physical world. Although his life is lived in the physical world or realm, the battle he fights is waged in the spiritual world (10:3). As such, the weapons that are used in that war are not physical weapons, but weapons that are divine in origin and power (cf. "Outfit the Right Armor"). These weapons lead to the destruction of everything that is set against God, even that which manifests itself in the lives of believers (10:5-6). What is Paul's point? Well, chapter ten introduces Paul's formal defense of his apostleship which is under attack and 10:1-6 in turn introduces chapter ten. Paul is arguing that although under attack himself, he recognizes the true nature of that attack. It is not first and foremost physical, but spiritual. He has maintained the right focus, and therefore is able to properly meet the challenges by attacking the right enemy.

Paul was a seasoned soldier, knowing well the enemy's battle strategies, so he was able to maintain the right focus in all his warring. Paul commends every Christian to have the same understanding of Satan's devices, "in order that no advantage be taken of us by Satan; for we are not ignorant of his schemes" (2 Cor. 2:11). In order to help yourself in dodging the distractions of life, refer to appendix six.

Chapter Five
THE ORIGIN AND NATURE OF MANKIND

"7. What do our standards teach as to the state of man at his creation?

... 1st. God created man in his own image. 2d. A reasonable and immortal soul endued with knowledge, righteousness, and true holiness, and placed in dominion over the creatures. 3d. Having God's law written on his heart and power to fulfill it, and yet under possibility of transgressing, being left to the freedom of his own will, which was subject to change.

The likeness of man to God respected – 1st. The kind of his nature; man was created like God a free, rational, personal Spirit. 2d. He was created like God as to perfection of his nature; in knowledge, Col. iii. 10; and righteousness and true holiness, Eph. iv. 24; and 3d. In his dominion over nature. Gen. i. 28."[9]

DOCTRINE

The essential area of concern here is that of the nature and character of man. Since many of the doctrinal areas being covered in this book deal with different parts of anthropology, that is the doctrine of man, this chapter will concentrate upon the matters that deal with the aspects of mankind's existence.

How Man Came into Existence

There are competing voices in our world today which are trying to postulate that mankind, rather than being a divine product, is nothing more than a naturalistic one. For example, Atheistic Evolution, one such false view, postulates that man was a result of natural causes. This theory contends that gradual changes occurred in organisms ascending from levels of less order to levels of greater order finally resulting in mankind. Theistic Evolution, another false view, argues that God guided the process of evolution. This hypothesis reasons that God chose to produce life through the mechanism of evolution. As we noted in the chapter entitled *The Holy Scripture*, "The Bible does not compete with any man-made source that might attempt to compete with it for equal hearing." The Bible unapologetically affirms that man was created by God, and this creation process was a miracle by God. By His word or decree, He created man. By a direct miracle of transformation of dust, God created man a living being (Gen.

1:26; 2:7; Ex. 20:11; Ps. 33:6-9; 148:1-5; Rom. 4:17; Col. 1:16; Heb. 11:3; Rev. 4:11).

Definition of Man and His Composition

Definition

It is clear from Genesis 1-2 that God did something special in the creation of mankind, in the generic sense of the word. Since man is a created being he must find out who he is from, the One who created him. However, mankind changed forever after Genesis 3 and therefore, if man as he was created to be is to be fully understood, we must define who he is from these first three chapters of the book of Genesis. It is in the events of the Garden of Eden that we discover who man really is.

With the above facts in mind, the following definition may be proposed. Man, a finite creation of God, is made dualistically in such a way that he reflects the nature of God as to His intellect, emotions, will, and dominion. As a result he was blessed, provided for by God, and commissioned by God to multiply, work, and rule the earth. Thus God has authority to restrict man's actions, blessing him for obedience and punishing him for disobedience.

Composition

Man is made up of both a material and an immaterial aspect. Both of these aspects play an important role in his existence and must of necessity relate to each other. The Bible makes definite statements about all three of these areas: 1) the material; 2) the immaterial; and 3) their relationship to each other.

Material

As to the material aspect of man, the Bible affirms that man is an earthly being (Gen. 2:7; 1 Cor. 15:47; 2 Cor. 4:7), of a unified composition (mind and body work together).

Immaterial

There are three important facts that should be noted about the immaterial aspect of mankind. First, the immaterial aspect of man finds its source in God. He was made in the image and likeness of God (Gen. 1:26-27; 2:7, 21-23). Second, as to the capacities of the image of God (called the *imago Dei*) in man, there are four aspects modeled from God, which are intellect (capabilities to reason in the intellectual realm), emotions (capabilities to experience in the realm of feelings), will (capabilities to choose in the ethical realm), and rule (capabilities to exercise dominion over the other realms of creation). Third, the transmission of the soul comes directly from a person's parents. The immaterial aspect of man is passed on naturally from both parents into the new life at the very point of conception. In Genesis 1, every created thing is endowed with the ability to reproduce itself after its own kind.[10]

Their Relationship

As to the nature of the material in relationship to the immaterial, the Bible affirms that the body is to be used to glorify God, the soul's expression of love and appreciation to its Creator. The body is good, in that it has come from the finger of God, although now it is stained with sin. Once it is remade, it will continue on into eternity with God (1 Cor. 6:19; 2 Cor. 5:10; Phil. 1:20; 1 Cor. 15:20-58; 1 Thess. 4:13-18).

Man's Pre-fall State

When God created man, in what state was he after God breathed the breath of life into his nostrils? There are two areas of consideration in regard to this question.

First, what were the capabilities of Adam? Relative to his intellect, he could understand, invent, and use language, which meant that he exhibited memory, and could think in symbols and concepts (Gen. 2:16, 20). He could also reason from ideas, concepts, and facts, to draw conclusions (Gen. 2:23, 24). Relative to his relationships, he was connected to animal life in that he had a physical body, but he was also separated from them in that he had an eternal soul and was a person. Relative to his function, he was commissioned by God for a specific duty. He was to work, subdue, and rule over all of God's created order (Gen. 1:26, 28).

Second, what were the moral qualities of man? Adam was created in holiness and moral goodness, due to the fact that he was God's creation in general (Gen. 1:31), and in God's image in specific (Gen. 1:27). Notice, Adam was not created neutral but positively holy, meaning that he was created with a disposition towards God and good. To be created neutral would not allow for a declaration of being good or evil. Yet Adam, although predisposed to the good, had the ability to choose evil. How do we explain this?

Understanding the difference between God and man can help us here. God is perfectly holy and unable to sin, He is sealed unto holy perfection. Man was endowed with God's free will, meaning the ability to choose between choices freely and without coercion. However, he was not endowed with the same degree of holiness as God possesses. In other words, the holiness of the divine nature is different than the holiness of a righteous contingent being, in that, unlike God, man was not sealed in holy perfection. This reality is validated for us in Genesis 3. After the fall of Adam into sin, God meted out the curses and clothed the fallen couple in garments of skin (vv. 14-21). After this takes place, the following statement is made, "'Behold, the man has become like one of Us, knowing good and evil; and now, lest he stretch out his hand, and take also from the tree of life, and eat, and live forever'—therefore the Lord God sent him out from the garden of Eden, to cultivate the ground from which he was taken" (vv. 22-23). The sealing of Adam's nature had not taken place previous to the events of chapter three. His removal from the Garden is a gracious act to prevent his nature from being permanently sealed in wickedness. Therefore, since he did not have the sealed holiness of

God, he was able to choose evil, although he was not evil himself.

Man's Fall

When man fell, he forever changed his destiny. In a very real sense his fall ended in Paradise Lost. The ramifications of the fall will be discussed in the chapter entitled *The Nature, Types, and Cure of Sin*. In this chapter the focus will be upon the temptation and the fall itself, without going extensively into its ramifications.

The Nature of the Temptation

What was the character of the temptation of man? Although man was made to have faith in the completely faithful God, the focus of the temptation deals with two questions. They are: *was man going to exercise faith in God for the process of attaining the knowledge of good and evil in the proper way, or was he going to subvert God's will for his own and obtain that knowledge the wrong way?* Notice, that God was not withholding the knowledge of good and evil from man, because he could have attained it one of two ways. If mankind had resisted temptation and exercised faith in God, he would have attained to the knowledge of good and evil through the means of resisting evil and choosing the good. However, if he did not resist the temptation but rather capitulated to it, he would also gain that knowledge by having chosen evil and rejected the good. That which is being withheld from man is not a body of factual knowledge (knowledge of **the** good and of **the** evil), but rather experiential harm (the knowledge of good and evil) (Gen. 2:17).[11] Adam chose the evil way and thus plunged the human race into death and eternal condemnation.

The Temptation's Methodology

The first attack that Satan attempts is to generate doubt in the mind of Eve by calling God's prohibition into question (Gen. 3:1-3). Notice that he misframes the question. He asks if God has limited them from eating of any tree at all. The implication is, if God denied access to any single tree, then He might as well have prohibited all of them. Satan paints God as unfair, when really He is extremely generous and good, only limiting one tree. He then moves to the total denial of what God has said (Gen. 3:4-5). The woman is then faced with the question: will she follow Satan, or will she follow God and her husband's prohibition? Satan's ploy is as follows: 1) Any restriction is not good; 2) God has restricted you in this area; 3) God's plan or order is not good; and 4) my unrestricted plan is good.[12]

APPLICATION

One of the commonly used definitions of the image of God in man was the one that was noted earlier under angelic being, which was the possession of intellect, emotions, will, and dominion. We also used this understanding in our discussion of the immaterial aspect of man. At that time it was noted that these elements referred to "intellect (capabilities to reason in the intellectual realm), emotions (capabilities to experience in the realm of feelings), will (capabilities to choose in the ethical realm), and rule (capabilities to exercise dominion over the other realms of creation)." The Bible directs the believer in each of these areas as to how he ought to live. Of the many conclusions that the Bible makes about these four areas and the believer's life, four of these conclusions are especially important for believers. The believer must possess: 1) A Mature Mind; 2) Controlled Emotions; 3) Control Over His Actions; and 4) A Sense of Responsible Stewardship.

A Mature Mind

In saying that the believer is to be a mature thinker, it is meant that he must position himself in such a context in which a developed thinking process will be cultivated. In 1 Corinthians 14:20 Paul says, "Brethren, do not be children in your thinking; yet in evil be babes, but in your thinking be mature." The point of this passage is that the believer has a responsibility to be mature in his thinking. The word "thinking" here signifies not just the ability to think, "but also to control one's thoughts or one's inner attitude of mind." Paul is preparing to instruct the Corinthians on a number of weighty, difficult issues regarding the practice and use of tongues, and he is attempting to prepare them by appealing to them to respond properly. Rather than reacting in a childish, irresponsible manner, he wants them to have a more stayed, controlled mental attitude in order to see the real significance of what he is saying. He therefore appeals to them to be mature in their thinking.

A believer who has a mature mind is able to take the truth of God, even the weightier more difficult aspects, and carefully think them through. Maturity is a lifelong quest for the believer and as such he is to pursue it from the time of his spiritual birth until such a time as he goes home to be with the Lord. This is why Paul could say of himself that he had not yet arrived at a point where he could coast, and neither had anyone else who considered themselves to be mature (Phil. 3:12-16). Maturity for the believer comes through a steady rejection of evil practices and a steady diet of the Word of God (1 Pet. 2:1-3).

Controlled Emotions

Placing our feelings in the right perspective is many times a difficult ordeal. In our culture, operating by feelings is common place, and in many ways is expected. The Bible, however, affirms that the believer acts on faith first, and allows his feelings to progress to the point of his faith, not vice versa. Therefore, what is the right use and perspective on emotions? Paul identifies one of the better uses of our emotions as our ability to empathize with one another. Paul says that the believer is to "Rejoice with those who rejoice and weep with those who weep" (Rom. 12:15). This command is given in the context of a series of commands having to do with the "one another" relationship between brothers and sisters in Christ. In such relationships the believer should seek to empathize, identify with, or understand other believers during times of joy, as well as in times of sorrow. By using two emotions that are diametrically opposed to each other, Paul is figuratively demonstrating that believers should identify with whatever another believer is going through, from joy to sorrow and anything in between.

Believers must commit to touching the lives of other believers through sharing with them in whatever times they are experiencing. Spiritual growth is not just concerned with bearing fruit for your own benefit, but also for the benefit of others as well. Important to this is the believer's ability to focus on the person of others (Mk. 12:31; Phil. 2:3), the needs of others (Rom. 12:13; 1 Jn. 3:17), and the interests of others (Phil. 2:4).

Disciplined Actions

Making the right choices is a part of the Christian life. How the believer acts clearly identifies who he is. Jesus makes it crystal clear that the believer has an obligation to conduct his life in conformity to the commandments or directives of His Savior. Jesus states in John 14:15, "If you love Me, you will keep My commandments." In this verse, loving God is equated with living according to Jesus' commands. This is the basis of Jesus' statement of the Great Commission which is the defining call on the believer's life. It reads, "Go therefore and make disciples of all the nations, baptizing them in the name of the Father and the Son and the Holy Spirit, *teaching them to observe all that I commanded you*; and lo, I am with you always, even to the end of the age" (Matt. 28:19-20, emphasis added). Keeping or following the commandments of Christ is imperative for the believer. The choices that a believer makes must fall in line with the dictates of the One to whom he has come for salvation.

Responsible Stewardship

Being a responsible steward is the obligation of every believer. The foundation of biblical stewardship is found in the physical commissioning of mankind in Genesis 1:28-30. After giving mankind his procreatory responsibilities (1:28) and his dietary responsibilities (1:29), God gave mankind his dominion responsibilities (1:30). In 1:28 God had indicated to mankind that he would be responsible to subdue the world and all that is in it. In that particular statement, God did not go further as to the duties of mankind as relative to the living things which were to be subdued. He addresses that issue in Genesis 1:30. In that verse, God indicates that animals, as man, are to be limited to a vegetarian diet. Here we see that part of what makes mankind mankind is his thoughtful responsibility for that which makes up his environment. This introduces the foundation of biblical stewardship. This foundation is widened as we progress through the Bible. As stewardship is related to the believer, the Bible teaches that not only his environment, but also his abilities (Rom. 12:3-6), his resources (1 Jn. 3:17; Jam. 2:14-17), and his time (Eph. 5:15-17) are to come under the control of God. The believer is responsible to bring each of these areas under the control, authority, and service of God. Our abilities are to be used for the benefit or ministry of others, our resources are to be used to meet the needs of others, and our time is to be used for the work of God.

Part Three

♦

God's Salvation

Sin, Christ, Salvation, and the Spirit
and Their Implications for Spiritual Growth

Chapter Six
THE NATURE, TYPES, AND CURE OF SIN

"Thus, then matters stood. The whole mass of the human race was under condemnation, was lying steeped and wallowing in misery, and was being tossed from one form of evil to another, and, having joined the faction of the fallen angels, was paying the well-merited penalty of that impious rebellion. For whatever the wicked freely do through blind and unbridled lust, and whatever they suffer against their will in the way of open punishment, this all evidently pertains to the just wrath of God. But the goodness of the Creator never fails either to supply life and vital power to the wicked angels (without which their existence would soon come to an end); or, in the case of mankind, who spring from a condemned and corrupt stock, to impart form and life to their seed, to fashion their members, and through the various seasons of their life, and in the different parts of the earth to quicken their senses, and bestow upon them the nourishment they need. For He judged it better to bring good out of evil, than not to permit any evil to exist. And if He had determined that in the case of men, as in the case of the fallen angels, there should be

no restoration to happiness, would it not have been quite just, that the being who rebelled against God, who in the abuse of his freedom spurned and transgressed the command of his Creator when he could so easily have kept it, who defaced in himself the image of his Creator by stubbornly turning away from His light, who by an evil use of his free-will broke away from his wholesome bondage to the Creator's laws, – would it not have been just that such a being should have been wholly and to all eternity deserted by God, and left to suffer the everlasting punishment he had so richly earned? Certainly so God would have done, had He been only just and not also merciful, and had He not designed that His unmerited mercy should shine forth the more brightly in contrast with the unworthiness of its objects."[13]

DOCTRINE

Sin is a term that is bandied-about in Christian circles, but that few take the time to really investigate as to what it means, what it does, and what should be done about it. In the Bible, sin is neither an ambiguous nor a vague term. As with most things having to do with God, He has spoken clearly and emphatically about it. The believer must attempt to understand its nature and, upon understanding it, take God's remedy for it. As such, this chapter's look at sin will encompass an analysis of what it is, including the different kinds mentioned or taught by the Bible, as well as a brief discussion of the remedy for each of the different kinds.

What Sin Is

In determining what sin is, our focus will be to attempt to arrive at a general conclusion as to its nature. Obviously sin is both a simple and a complex doctrine at the same time. As such, we will attempt to look at the doctrine of sin from both a simple and a complex perspective. What follows is a short analysis of what the Bible speaks of regarding sin generally, as to its nature. Sin may be defined as any act which violates the character or law of God, whereby it exceeds or is deficient of the moral law or essential character of God. Such violations may be of omission or commission. Sins of omission mean not being or doing what God requires, while the sins of commission are doing those things which God forbids. Whatever the situation, sin is considered as being directed against God, whether it be overt or not.

Sin is moral and ethical in its nature (Lev. 4:2, 27; 6:2; Rom. 4:15; 7:13; 1 Jn. 3:4; 5:17). It is absolute as to its value, meaning there is not a neutrality in sin. Either an act is good or it is evil, it is not between the two. This is so because of the nature of good and evil, they both exclude each other, as does light and dark.

Sin further encompasses guilt and pollution, that is, one stands in a state of guilt because of who he is, and because of what he does, and one is polluted in that he is corrupted (Rom. 3:9-20). Sin has as its source the individual's heart, that is, the central organ of the soul (speaking on the immaterial level) from which decisions and contemplations of actions take place.

By way of summary, sin is any non-conformity to the character and standards of God, either in act, disposition, or state. Sin will be discussed under three basic headings: original sin, imputed sin, and actual sin.

Kinds of Sin

In order to fully elaborate on sin, theologians have isolated three primary hubs that control and propel the discussions. These hubs are original sin, imputed sin, and actual sin. The previous discussion of the nature of sin, will suffice to inform us on actual sin. The following discussion will therefore concentrate on original and imputed sin.

Original Sin

The question that original sin attempts to answer is what is the state of man as he enters the world, or what is the state of man post–fall. His state is called original sin, because it finds its source in the original or first man, Adam (Rom. 5:12-21). Also, it is called original because it is the root of sinfulness in mankind. Original sin is that state of existence affecting the totality of man's being, including but not limited to his intellect, will, emotions, and dominion. Into this state all men are conceived and thus born. It determines their nature as sinful, evil, and corrupted. Therefore all of mankind is worthy of just condemnation by God.

This is also termed hereditary sin, because it is the sin nature with which we are born. By using hereditary, the means of its transmission is clearly outlined. When Adam and Eve fell they became corrupted morally, or in other words they died spiritually, meaning they could no longer function in the spiritual realm (Eph. 2:1-10). Since God created humanity to procreate only individuals after their own kind, Adam and Eve were only able to reproduce spiritually dead people (Ps. 51:5).

The doctrine of original sin can be more clearly understood by looking at its outcome, that is, what results in man from the reality of original sin.

Man is Absolutely Condemned

This speaks to the guilt of mankind. Man stands guilty before God because of who he is by his nature. When we say that man is guilty, it is meant that he is culpable or blameworthy. Psalm 51:5 indicates that such guilt is something with which one is born. Romans 3:9-20 indicates that guilt is based upon who man is, referring to his nature (3:10-11), and what man does, referring to his actions (3:13-18). Guilt incurs punishment or judgment. The punishment incurred by man for his guilt is that of judgment in hell (Rom. 6:23).

Man is Absolutely Deficient

When it is said that man is absolutely deficient, it means that man has no righteousness of his own. In other words, man lacks original righteousness. Since man does not have any righteousness, it can be justly said that there is no good (morally speaking) in man. Romans 3:10-12 declares that man does not have goodness in his state, and does not do good things. Why is this the case? The only type of good actions that God accepts are actions that are good in outward performance and good in motive (cf. 1 Sam. 15:1-23). In other words, they must align themselves with God's directions and be of the right motives. For an action to be considered good, biblically speaking, the motive must be to glorify God (cf. 1 Cor. 10:31). The only individuals who perform such deeds are saved people. While man is significant, due to the image of God in him, this image has been completely affected by sin to the point that he no longer possesses any righteousness of his own. Since righteousness must be reckoned to man, he must not possess any of his own. In reference to righteousness, he is completely bankrupt. God says of him in his fallen state that "every intent of the thoughts of his heart was only evil continually" (Gen. 6:5). Righteousness is no longer part of his nature.

Man is Absolutely Wicked (Inclined to Evil)

Next it can be said that man is absolutely wicked. When it is said that man is absolutely wicked, it means man is inclined towards evil, as Genesis 6:5 clearly indicates. In other words, he possesses positive evil. Mankind is pre-disposed to doing evil. This is related to man's absolute deficiency, but speaks to what replaces righteousness in his life. Because he is bankrupt of righteousness, and because he is not light, he must be dark, for there is no grey in the Bible. God clearly recognizes this fact in Genesis 6:5 and 8:21. Both passages squarely teach that mankind is completely consumed with doing evil. It is what drives his actions. In Biblical terms, he loves the darkness (evil) and hates the light (good) (Jn. 3:19-21). Man's inclination towards God was replaced with an inclination towards evil when Adam sinned in the garden. Man is moved or energized towards behaving in a manner inconsistent with God's character (His nature) and law (His commands).

Man is Absolutely Dead (Inability)

The natural result of the preceding three outcomes is that man is absolutely dead. By absolutely dead it is meant that man possesses total inability. What is meant by total inability? Total inability means that man is completely unable to do anything that would meet with God's approval, and that man is completely unable to change his disposition towards sin, to loving God, or begin himself down such a path (cf. Isa. 64; Jn. 6:41-44; 10:22-30). Man cannot rescue himself from his condition, nor can he assist in such a process. No clearer reason for this can be given than the words of Paul found in Ephesians 2:1-3. There we learn that man is dead in his trespasses and sin. To be dead means to no longer have the capabilities to operate or function in the realm in which the death occurs. So physical death means to no longer have the ability to function in the physical realm. Spiritual death, thus, means no longer having the ability to function in the spiritual realm. Dead men cannot believe in God. Therefore, Paul tells us that faith, as is the whole salvation process, is a gift from God (Eph. 2:8). Without God man cannot come to God at all. If you are a saved person, it is because God, unassisted in the process, moved in your life and drew you to Himself; and you received what He did.

Imputed Sin

Imputed means to place on one's account, or to reckon to one. Imputed sin seeks to deal with the connection of Adam's sin with the human race. How is his sin transmitted to us? While some deny that there are any connections, one wonders if they have ever read Romans 5:12-21. The issue is not if we are connected, but how we are connected. Imputed sin indicates that the human race was justly punished and cursed by God for Adam's sin with the result that Adam's guilt was reckoned to or placed on our accounts before God. The question still remains, however, as to how this occurred, or on what basis it occurred.

Two primary answers have been put forward to explain the relationship: 1) the seminal or realistic view; and 2) the federal or representative view. The seminal view says that each member of the human race was contained in Adam and as such when Adam sinned all of us were sinning along with him. However, why not hold that the human race is accountable for all of Adam's sin, not just one? Further, everyone has a distinctive personality, we are not a mass of humanity. Hebrews 7:9-10, which is usually used in support of this view, says nothing regarding sin's transmission. For these reasons the federal or representative view seems clearly to be the best one. It states that Adam was the designated representative of the whole human race, so that when he sinned, his condemnation was the condemnation of all (Rom. 5:12-21).

The Remedy for Sin

God's basic remedy for sin is that of forgiveness and cleansing, but each type of sin carries with it its own special cure. The remedy for personal sin is that of sanctifying forgiveness, that is, forgiveness that is part of the sanctification process and not the justification process. The unbeliever is forgiven of his sins when he receives Christ as his personal Savior, removing the guilt of these sins, which is justifying forgiveness. The believer is forgiven of his sins when he prays and asks forgiveness from God, not for the purpose of salvation, but for the purpose of re-opening channels of communication and fellowship, which is sanctifying forgiveness.

The remedy for original sin is three-fold. It provides for both the fact of original sin, as well as its ramifications. First, the unbeliever is redeemed, which includes a judgment of the sin nature by Christ on the cross, so that he no longer has to serve sin, but can now serve Christ (Rom. 6:1-11; Gal. 5:25). Second, he is given the gift of the Holy Spirit which allows him to walk in the Spirit and not satisfy the sinful desires, which still exist, since he is still encased in his old body, with its passions and desires (Rom. 7:7-17; Gal. 5:16-24). Third, he is to be resurrected or transformed in the rapture, so that the last vestiges of the old man that he was will be completely removed (1 Jn. 3:1-2).

The remedy for imputed sin is imputed righteousness. That is, the sinner has the righteousness of Christ imputed or reckoned to him at the moment of salvation (Rom. 5:12-21).

APPLICATION

Sin is obviously one of the major hindrances of spiritual growth in the life of the believer. Not only does it affect our relationship with God, but it affects our relationship to ourselves, as well as to other believers. The believer struggles against the sin tendencies that are part of his earthly existence all his life. Sin has taken up permanent residency in us until our resurrection, so we must be sure not to fall prey to unresisted, unrelinquished, unresolved sin if we are going to grow in the manner in which God desires.

The Dangers of Unresisted Sin

By unresisted sin it is meant sins which exploit one's weaknesses, sins that many times, rather than being resisted, are toyed with. As was demonstrated in the previous chapter, man is a unique being. Unlike any of God's other creatures, he possesses elements that are uniquely his. This uniqueness stretches even to each individual person. Each individual man or woman has unique characteristics all his own. Further, in studying angels it became clear that Satan is a master schemer and strategist, planning the most strategic way to bring the believer down. Satan recognizes those special areas of weakness in each believer's life and develops his attacks appropriately. The author of Hebrews, realizing these truths, in Hebrews 12:1 makes the following statement, "Therefore, since we have so great a cloud of witnesses surrounding us, let us also lay aside every encumbrance, and the sin which so easily entangles us, and let us run with endurance the race that is set before us."[14] In a believer's life there may very well be a sin which "so easily entangles" him. A sin that the believer has a particularly difficult time resisting. Knowing this and particularly guarding himself from it allows the believer to run the race of the Christian life more effectively.

The answer for the believer is focusing on Jesus Christ, which allows him to not lose heart and grow weary. The author of Hebrews lists three things in Hebrews 12:2-3 that entail focusing on Jesus: 1) Jesus as our Perfecter; 2) Jesus as the Patient Endurer; and 3) Jesus as the Victor. Each of these elements can help the believer in his walk. Jesus, the Perfecter, tells the believer that God is going to complete the work He has begun in the Christian (Phil. 1:16). Jesus, the Patient Endurer, communicates that believers must also patiently endure in their battle with sin. Jesus, the Victor, indicates to the believer that he too can gain victory in his walk with God.

The Dangers of Unrelinquished Sin

Sin must be resisted, but it must also be relinquished in the believer's life. It is to be the abnormal situation for the believer to be living a life of perpetual sin. We are to relinquish sin. Paul speaks to these issues in the eighth chapter of Romans. Romans 8:4 says, "in order that the requirement of the Law might be fulfilled in us, who do not walk according to the flesh, but according to the Spirit." Having explained, in the previous three verses, how the condemnation of mankind is removed from the believer, Paul moves on to indicate the purpose for which the liberation took place. The apostle begins by giving the nature of that purpose.

The purpose for the liberation was in order that the requirements of the Law might be fulfilled in believers. When one is found to be in accordance with the law, he is acquitted of any wrong doing. This speaks to a positive judicial rendering, in other words, justification. When believers were liberated, that liberation was not a liberation to do and behave in any way they wanted, it was a liberation that enabled them to be pronounced as having abided in the law. The focus here is not how you live, but the judicial statement of God regarding your righteous standing based on Christ's work. Since we could not in ourselves fulfill the law, Christ came and fulfilled the law Himself, since the law could not condemn Him because of His perfect life. His fulfillment of the law was then applied to us through the life producing Spirit, resulting in us not having to be condemned by the law.

One might ask, to whom does this justification apply? According to Paul, the answer would be "those that walk or behave in a certain fashion." Before Paul looks at who it applies to, he first alerts the Romans to those to whom it does not apply. Anyone who walks by the flesh evidences that the law has not been fulfilled in him, he says. If, on the other hand, the person walks according to the Spirit, he evidences that the law has been fulfilled in him. To walk means to conduct your life. Therefore, the person who walks according to the flesh is the person who carries out in conduct those things dictated by the flesh, while the person who walks according to the Spirit is the person who carries out in conduct those things dictated by the Spirit.

At this point in his argument, Paul has alerted the Romans to the intricate, inseparable nature of justification and sanctification. Justification is the act of God whereby He pronounces the regenerated sinner righteous in His sight, based on the sacrifice of Christ and our exercise of faith in Him. Sanctification is that act of God whereby He progressively makes the regenerated sinner righteous, which is a continual process while he is in a non-glorified state, and to which the believer responds with obedience and love of Christ. While the two can be discussed separately, they are not experienced separately.

What Paul is communicating is that those who have been justified, are those who walk according to the Spirit. In Paul's presentation there are only two types of people, those who walk according to the flesh, and those who walk according to the Spirit. Someone might ask, what about the person who is justified but does not walk according to the Spirit? Understand that Paul is presenting normative Christianity. Those who are justified and do not walk according to the Spirit, are living a perversion of Christianity. The unified voice of the New Testament is that justified Christians walk or conduct their lives by the Spirit. It is to be the grotesquely abnormal situation in which a born again Christian does not conduct himself by the Spirit. You might say, "Well, I just don't know how to walk in the Spirit." There is no excuse for not walking in the Spirit, and because God has given us His Word, any excuse which would be given would be deemed unacceptable. Further, there are churches and ministries that are geared for the very purpose of instruction in God's Word. God will not excuse lack of effort on our part.

Lest we are confused on what walking or conducting our lives in the Spirit means, Paul engages this particular discussion in the next seven verses (Rom. 8:5-11). The focus of this passage is being controlled by the Spirit. The people who walk by the Spirit are those who concentrate on the things of the Spirit and by so doing, experience life and peace. The people who walk by the flesh do so because they are concentrating on the things of the flesh which manifests themselves in death. This is due to the fact that such a state is hostility to God and is manifested by not keeping His will, thereby not pleasing Him. Those who concentrate on the Spirit, on the other hand, do so because they are indwelt by the Holy Spirit, who will ultimately grant them life.

The Dangers of Unresolved Sin

Unlike wine and some types of cheese, sin does not get better with age. When a believer allows sin to ferment in his life, he reaps disastrous consequences for his lack of spiritual growth and advancement. Psalm 32 provides a picturesque backdrop for a discussion of the dangers of unresolved sin. The Psalm itself is about the blessedness of forgiveness, but in the midst of this Psalm, David speaks to the issue of what his life was like when he did not resolve his sin with God. This discussion is begun in Psalm 32:3. David said that when he did not confess his sin, there were three results: 1) he was physically deteriorating through his mental torment (32:3); 2) God resisted and heavily convicted him (32:4a); and 3) his physical energy was drained from him (32:4b). It is only through a three-fold process of *acknowledging* (owning up to his sin before God), *revealing* (being honest with God about his sin), and *confessing* (agreeing with God about his sin) his sin to God that David found the physical, mental, and spiritual replenishing and invigoration that enabled him to re-establish his walk with God (32:5c-7). The believer with unresolved sin in his life must do the same, if he is to re-establish himself with God.

Chapter Seven
THE PERSON AND WORK OF JESUS CHRIST

"I believe in one GOD THE FATHER Almighty; Maker of heaven and earth, and of all things visible and invisible.

And in one Lord JESUS CHRIST, the only-begotten Son of God, begotten of the Father before all worlds [God of God], Light of Light, very God of very God, begotten, not made, being of one substance [essence] with the Father; by whom all things were made; who, for us men and for our salvation, came down from heaven, and was incarnate by the Holy Ghost of the Virgin Mary, and was made man; and was crucified also for us under Pontius Pilate, he suffered and was buried; and the third day he rose again, according to the Scriptures; and ascended into heaven, and sitteth on the right hand of the Father; and he shall come again, with glory, to judge both the quick and the dead; whose kingdom shall have no end.

And [I believe] in the Holy Ghost, the Lord and Giver of Life; who proceedeth from the Father [and the Son]; who with the Father and the Son together is worshiped and glorified; who spake by the Prophets. And [I believe] one Holy Catholic and Apostolic

Church. I acknowledge one Baptism for the remission of sins; and I look for the resurrection of the dead, and the life of the world to come. Amen."[15]

DOCTRINE

The focus of this chapter is what is theologically referred to as Christology. In beginning a doctrinal investigation into who Christ is, one qualification should be mentioned to delineate the exact direction of the discussion. Since the person of Christ is also addressed when talking about the Godhead and salvation, it is necessary to distinguish what is said here from what is said of Him under other doctrinal areas.

When discussing the Godhead, the aspect of Christ's existence that is examined is His relationship to the other Trinitarian Persons, God the Father and God the Holy Spirit. On the other hand when looking at the existence of Christ in reference to salvation, the examination focuses on His work in providing redemption for mankind. As such, the focus here in reference to the doctrinal area of Christology is placed upon the existence of Christ in the Pre-incarnate and Incarnate modes of His existence, as well as His functions in these modes. This chapter will focus on the second and third areas.

The Nature of Christ

The fact that the pre-incarnate Son of God, the second person in the Trinity, became flesh cannot be denied (Jn. 1:1-

18; 1 Jn. 1:1-4). The incarnation is the center piece of any discussion dealing with Jesus Christ. Incarnation means *"in the flesh"*. To understand it, we must look at two of its important aspects: the means of the incarnation and the result of the incarnation.

The means of the incarnation was the virgin birth, which was accomplished by God, and was a sign of Christ's uniqueness (Mt. 1:18-25; Lk.1:26-38; 2:1-7). Dr. Charles Ryrie in his book entitled *Basic Theology* lists six important things that grew out of the incarnation. They were: 1) God could be revealed to us (Jn. 1); 2) salvation could be provided for us (Rom. 1:3-5; 3-5); 3) an example to follow could be provided for us (1 Cor. 11:1; 1 Pet. 2:21-25; 1 Jn. 2:6); 4) the works of Satan could be destroyed (1 Jn. 3:8); 5) Christ could be recognized as a sympathetic high priest (Heb. 4:14); and 6) Christ could be recognized as a qualified judge (Jn. 5:22, 27).

As to the nature or outcome of the incarnation, the church of Jesus Christ has not been silent. The true church believes that Jesus Christ is completely God, possessing all the attributes of deity, as well as its prerogatives (Jn. 1:1-8; 10:22-39; Col. 1:13-23; Heb. 1:1-14). He is also completely man, in that He took on human form with all its limitations and passions (except for the evil ones), except sin (Mt. 4:2; Lk. 2:52; Jn. 4:6; Phil. 2:5-11). His natures, divine and human, are perfectly united, but are not co-mingled, or mixed, and remain with Him from the point of His incarnation into eternity (Ac. 7:54-56; Rev. 19:11-19). Such a union allows Him to be just one person, possessing the attributes of both natures, in such a way that it might be said that these attributes belong to this single person.[16] Finally, the person of Christ is not a new one, meaning He did not come into being in the womb of Mary. Rather the person of Christ is that of the eternal God, who in space and time took on the nature of a man, and evermore exists in such a nature, being deity (Jn. 8:48-59; 17:5, 24).[17]

The Sinlessness of Christ

Peter refers to Christ as "a lamb unblemished and spotless" (1 Pet. 1:19; cf. Jn. 1:29). The author of Hebrews indicates that Christ was "without sin" (Heb. 4:15). But how does one reconcile Christ's sinlessness with His temptation? After all, the same author who indicated that Christ was "without sin" is the same author who prior to that says, He was "tempted in all things as we are" (Heb. 4:15). Because sin is something that is associated with mankind, what relationship does it have to Christ, and what effect does such a relationship have on His deity? Although the sinlessness of Christ is sometimes viewed as a moot point, its importance cannot be ignored by the Christian.

Two primary solutions have developed that attempt to answer these questions and reconcile the above truths: 1) the peccability of Christ; and 2) the impeccability of Christ. Both positions end up at the same conclusion, Christ was without sin both in His actions and His character, but they get to their conclusions different ways.

The first position, the peccability of Christ, argues that Christ was sinless, but He was able to sin. His sinlessness was a result of His resisting sin's onslaught. The second position, the impeccability of Christ, argues that Christ was sinless, because He was not able to sin. Thus, either Christ was able to sin and chose not to (peccability), or He was not able to sin at all (impeccability).

Those who hold to the peccability of Christ argue that for a temptation to be a temptation the one being tempted must at least be able to succumb to it. However, there are two problems with this position. First, the ability to sin alludes to an innate susceptibility to sin, either a deficiency or an incompleteness, neither of which is a reality in reference to the God-man. Second, it does not fully take into account His deity (though this view many times does not do so purposefully). Since Christ was very God of very God in union with man, then it would be impossible for Him to be able to sin, just as it is for God. Granted, He has two natures, but He is only one person. His human nature cannot act independently of the divine.

Those who hold to the impeccability of Christ simply argue that the classification of a temptation as a temptation lies not in the temptee, but the tempter. This means that Christ could be assailed, attacked, or solicited to sin (since He had a human nature), but it was impossible for Him to succumb to that temptation, since His human will was united with the divine will. Adam fell, not because he had a sin nature, but because of a choice of his will to sin, the ability of such a choice could not exist in the God-man. Although Adam was positively holy, or inclined towards holiness, his will was not in union or tied to an infinitely holy character, which would have made him unable to sin, but such was the case with Christ.[18]

The Work of Christ

Christ, as do all the members of the Trinity, has a particular function. The function or work of Christ is usually discussed under the designation of the office of Christ. The office of Christ was threefold. He functions as prophet, priest, and king. Christ is the only person to ever hold all three of these offices at the same time. Some prophets were priests, some kings prophesied, but no one ever served in all three capacities.[19]

The role of the prophet was to proclaim the message of God to the people of God. He stood between God and man, and spoke to man from God. God put His words in the mouth of the prophet (Deut. 18:15-22). As prophet, Christ proclaimed the message of God in His preaching and teaching (Mt. 21:11; Mk. 1:38; Lk. 7:16). This function was predicted in the Old Testament (Isa. 61:1) and Christ fulfilled the prophetic office throughout His ministry, whether to His disciples or the multitudes; and it was authoritative (Mt. 11:5; Lk. 4:14-20; 24:19; Jn. 4:19; 6:14; 7:40). His major message was that repentance was necessary because the kingdom of God was at hand (Mt. 4:17; Mk. 1:14-15). Jesus referred to Himself as a prophet (Lk. 13:33). When the kingdom was rejected by the Jews, the message turned to focus on the establishment of the church (Mt. 16:13-20). When the church is raptured, He will continue His work with the Jews. By His very nature He is the spoken Word of God (Heb. 1:1-2). As such He forevermore preaches.

If the prophet speaks the message of God to man, the priest talks to God on behalf of man. He represents sinful man to God. It is the role of the priest to be a channel for man accessing God. He regulates man's behavior before God and his entrance to God (Deut. 33:8-11; cf. Mal. 1:6-2:9). Christ's role as priest was also prophesied in the Old Testament (Ps. 110:4; Isa. 53:12; Zech. 6:12; Lk. 23:34; Heb. 6:19). As priest, Christ gave a sacrifice for those He represents (Isa. 53:1-9; Jn. 1:29; Heb. 10:10-12; Rev. 5:6). He also serves as the medium through which approach can be made to God (Heb. 4:14-16). He further functions as an Advocate between the believer and God when the believer is accused and is worthy of punishment (Rom. 8:34; 1 Jn. 2:1-2). All of these are priestly functions. Probably the most crucial for believers is one attribute of His priesthood that is unlike earthly priests. He is an eternal priest, and therefore, He can do these priestly functions forever for those He has redeemed (1 Tim. 2:5; Heb. 7:22-25; 1 Jn. 2:1).

The king is God's vice regent. He rules on behalf of God, over the people of God. As was the case in the previous two functions, so it is with this one; it was prophesied in the Old Testament (Ps. 2:6; 132:11; Jer. 23:5; Ez. 37:24; Mt. 2:5-6; Lk. 1:32; Jn. 1:49; Jn. 18:33-37). As king, Christ serves as sovereign regent over, not just the universe, but also God's promised future kingdom on the earth (Psa. 110:1-3; Isa. 9:6-7; 1 Cor. 15:20-28; Rev. 20:1-6).

The Glory of Christ

The glory of Christ is a crucial element of who we believe He was and is, for it has to do with the acceptance of what He did, said, and who He was and remains to be. It is the cosmic validation of Christ. As Christ neared the end of His life and ministry on the earth, He spoke often of His glorification (Jn. 12:28; 13:31-32; 17:4). It was obviously important to Him, so it should be important to us. Christ's glory includes His resurrection, ascension, and enthronement next to God in Heaven. This process only came after He had accomplished all that He had come to do (Jn. 12:23-36; 17:22-26). It was the natural outcome of His humility and sacrifice (Phil. 2:6-11), validating that He was sent by God and accomplished what He was sent to do (Jn. 12:23-36; 17:22-26; Heb. 1:3). So important is it that Paul says that if the resurrection (the key to Christ's glorification) of Christ did not occur, then the Christian faith is a fraud and invalid (1 Cor. 15:12-19).

APPLICATION

A sign could be placed over the head of every Christian which would simply read, "**UNDER CONSTRUCTION BY THE HOLY TRINITY, GENERAL CONTRACTOR.**" The believer in a very real sense is under construction. God is in the process of rebuilding him. But into what is the believer being built? Most simply put, the believer is being made into the image of Jesus Christ. The Archetype of spiritual growth is Jesus Christ. In other words, we are to copy or look like Him. Of the many implications of this statement, three serve as foundational and highly imperative for spiritual growth. They are: 1) Christ's Imputation; 2) Christ's Imitation; and 3) Christ's Intention. Each of these plays an important role in our spiritual growth.

Christ's Imputation

Christ's imputation deals with how we became what we are today, sinners who have been born again, that is, sinners saved by grace through faith alone. In a very real sense it tells us how we were started on this climb of spiritual growth in the first place. Romans chapter five clearly teaches the believer the basis of what he is. Romans 5:1-11 informs the believer of the results or benefits of justification. Romans 5:12-21 informs the believer as to the divine means of justification, that is, imputation. We are declared righteous based on the fact that Christ has imputed to the believer His own righteousness through faith. The essence of Christ's imputation is that God transferred to believers, who had the penalty of sin from Adam (5:12-14), the righteousness of Christ (5:15-17, **19**). Death was the physical sign and result of the fact of spiritual death, which was attributed to all men because of Adam's sin. Adam was mankind's federal head, and when he sinned, the guilt and penalty of his sin was imputed to or reckoned to the account of all mankind. So, although there was no law prior to Moses, there was death due to Adam's sin (5:12-14).

The free gift of Christ, based on the grace of God, was imputed to many, that is, those who ". . . receive the abundance of grace and of the gift of righteousness . . ." (5:15-17, 19). That is, Christ's righteousness has been consigned to us, making us alive in Him. Therefore, the believer now owes his very life to Christ, and must be willing to give his life for Him. Paul puts it this way in Romans 8:12, "So then, brethren, we are under obligation, not to the flesh, to live according to the flesh *. . . but to the Spirit (the medium of imputation), to live according to the Spirit*" (emphasis and parenthesis added).

Christ's Imitation

Christ's imitation speaks to the fact that the attitude of the believer should be to imitate the Lord Jesus Christ in his behavior. This is a constant theme throughout the New Testament and forms an integral part of spiritual growth. The New Testament views everything in the believer's life as an aspect of following Christ. Christ Himself began this principle by indicating that true discipleship is signified by a willingness to and an actual lifestyle of imitating Him (Mt. 16:24). The lifestyle of imitation carries on from the point of salvation through our ultimate glorification, which will be seen in the next section.

This imitation can be mediated through another as indicated in Paul's thought on this subject. In drawing his discussion of the believer's liberty to an end, Paul brings up the idea of imitation (1 Cor. 8:1-10:33). Paul uses this idea as a means of exhorting and encouraging believers to have an *others* sense about them. As such, he urges them, the Corinthians, to follow him in his pursuit of Christ (1 Cor. 11:1). A similar theme is taught by Peter, except his usage of Christ's example is in the arena of suffering. Peter's contention is that believers are to walk "in His steps" in reference to suffering in this life (1 Pet. 2:21).

The common thread throughout each of these examples is that Christ forms the archetype of the believer's walk on the earth. He is the ultimate **end** to which we should strive, therefore He is also the **means** of getting there. No doubt this is why the author of Hebrews says, "let us run with endurance the race that is set before us, fixing our eyes on Jesus, the author and perfecter of faith" (12:1d-2b).

Christ's Intention

The focus of Christ's intention springs from the previous category of Christ's imitation. Christ's ultimate goal for the believer is to make the believer look like Him. Paul expounds this idea in Romans 8 and 2 Corinthians 3. In Romans 8, Paul informs the believer he has been "predestined to become conformed to the image of His Son" (Rom. 8:29). Part of God's selection of the believer is related to His goal. Not only has God ordained the believer to salvation and ordained the means for the believer to be saved, He also ordains the goal for which believers are chosen.[20]

Moving from the fact of Christ's intention, the Bible also speaks of the process of Christ's intention. In 2 Corinthians 3, Paul, in coming to the end of his discussion on the difference between the old covenant (Mosaic Law) and the new covenant (the covenant of the Spirit), indicates that the believer is being transformed into the image of Christ in stages of ever increasing glory (vv. 17-18). That being the case, the believer has an obligation to participate in the transformation process now. John speaks to this very issue in his first epistle. In 1 John 3:2 John explains to the readers that the child of God does not yet know what he is going to be like, because it has not yet been revealed to him. Knowledge of the future is limited for the believer, but he need not worry because he knows the one who orders the future (Eccl. 7:14). Although he does not have this experiential knowledge, he does conceptually know that he is going to look like Christ when Christ appears to him (1 Jn. 3:2). That being the case, John says in 3:3, "everyone who has this hope fixed on Him purifies himself, just as He is pure." The idea here is that if we know that we are going to be like Him in the future, we need to begin the process of pursuing that likeness now on the earth. Since Christ is pure, we must seek to be pure now.

Chapter Eight
THE BASIS AND MEANS OF SALVATION

"Lastly, There may be wonderful moving of the affections, in souls that are not at all touched with regenerating grace. Where there is no grace, there may, notwithstanding, be a flood of tears, as in Esau, "who found no place of repentance, though he sought it carefully with tears" (Heb. 12:17). There may be great flashes of joy; as in the hearers of the Word, represented in the parable by the stony ground, who "anon with joy receive it" (Matt. 13:20). There may also be great desires after good things, and great delight in them too; as in those hypocrites described in Isa. 58:2: "Yet they seek Me daily, and delight to know My ways: they take delight in approaching to God." See how high they may sometimes stand, who yet fall away (Heb. 6:4-6). They may be "enlightened, taste of the heavenly gift," be "partakers of the Holy Ghost, taste of the good Word of God, and the powers of the world to come." Common operations of the Divine Spirit, like a land flood, make a strange turning of things upside down: but when they are over, all runs again in the ordinary channel. All these things may be, where the

sanctifying Spirit of Christ never rests upon the soul, but the stony heart still remains; and in that case these affections cannot but wither, because they have no root.

But regeneration is a real thorough change, whereby the man is made a new creature (2 Cor. 5:17). The Lord God makes the creature a new creature, as the goldsmith melts down the vessel of dishonor, and makes it a vessel of honor. Man is, in respect of his spiritual state, altogether disjointed by the fall; every faculty of the soul is, as it were, dislocated: in regeneration the Lord loosens every joint, and sets it right again. Now this change made in regeneration, is:

1. *A change of qualities or dispositions: it is not a change of the substance, but of the qualities of the soul. Vicious qualities are removed, and the contrary dispositions are brought in, in their room. "The old man is put off" (Eph. 4:22); "the new man put on" (ver. 24).*
2. *It is a supernatural change; he that is born again, is born of the Spirit (John 3:5).*
3. *It is a change into the likeness of God. "We, beholding, as in a glass, the glory of the Lord, are changed into the same image" (2 Cor. 3:18).*
4. *It is a universal change; "all things become new" (2 Cor. 5:17)."*[21]

DOCTRINE

The focus of the Doctrine of Salvation is the work that God performed in giving life to unregenerate man. Reversing the ramifications of Adam's sin took a divine act, and this act is at the heart of what makes Christianity distinctive. All that we have studied to this point will intersect in this study. Soteriology, the theological term given to the study of salvation, seeks to explain all the different aspects of the divine act of salvation, and place it in reference to God's other divine works. In our study of Salvation we will look at the nature of the atonement, the medium of salvation, as well as the different roles of the members of the Godhead in salvation.

The Definition of Salvation

Salvation is that act of God whereby He takes one who is a sinner both by nature and by actions (Rom. 1:18-3:20), which have rightly condemned him to eternal punishment in hell because he stands in opposition to the righteousness and holiness of God (Eph. 2:1-3), and delivers him from that just condemnation through the work of His blessed Son (Mark 10:45). His Son suffered in the sinner's place upon the cross atop Golgotha's hill, the punishment due the sinner (2 Cor. 5:21; 1 Pet. 3:18). Such suffering placed the sinner in right (or righteous) standing before God (2 Cor. 5:18-19). He did this by justifying him (pronouncing him righteous), sanctifying him (progressively making him righteous), and glorifying him (permanently sealing him in righteousness), through the medium of election and faith (Rom. 9:1-24; Eph. 2:4-10), being carried out by the Holy Spirit.

The One Necessary To Provide Salvation

At the heart of the above definition is the type of person needed to save us from this rightful condemnation. This question naturally overlaps the study of Christ (chapter seven) and as such some truths which were already mentioned will be mentioned without much elaboration.

Since those who are to be saved, or redeemed, are mankind, it is then necessary that the one who redeems them be a man also (Heb. 2:14-17). The one who saves us, must of necessity take our place, and suffer our condemnation, to pay the price and meet God's righteous standard.

Not only must the one who redeems man be a man himself, but he must also be God, if he is to supply the salvation of which man is in need. There is a tension that arises regarding the work that the person would have to accomplish. Since all men are tarnished by sin and defilement due to the fall, no man can serve as a perfectly holy sacrifice. Further, since the punishment for sin is eternal condemnation or judgment and the sins are innumerable, then the one who must suffer must be able to suffer infinitely. Also, since the standards that are to be met are God's, the one who meets those standards must be as good as God. Therefore, the only one able to meet God's standards in such a way as has been described is God Himself. There is just one problem, however, God is not man. Therefore, for us to be saved, God must become man. In Him becoming man, however, He must become all man, meaning He must have a complete and full human nature (this does not necessitate sin, because it was a later addition to man; in other words it is not necessary to be by nature a sinner to be fully man). Yet He must also remain totally and completely God, in order to meet God the Father's righteous standard. Thus He must be very God of very God, and very man of very man. Christian teachers and theologians have called this the hypostatic union (Mt. 1:21; Ro. 1:1-8; Phil. 2:5-11).[22] Jesus is the God-man.

The Nature of the Atonement

Having discussed the one who had to supply salvation, it is now important to investigate what was accomplished in that provision. Here we will consider what exactly was accomplished by Christ's atonement. As to His death specifically, several biblical terms and concepts have been used to describe what was accomplished in and through Christ's death. The atonement is an extensive topic in Scripture, covering a multiplicity of topics and passages. What follows is a list of some of the terms used to explain the atonement with a short explanation of each:

Atonement–to cover sin; a general term used to encapsulate all of the work of Christ.[23]

Expiation–God's act of removing the guilt and sin of man by Christ's suffering punishment in the sinner's place (Rom. 3:25-26; 1 Pet. 3:18).

Forgiveness and Remission—Divine absolving of the sinner of his sinful offense made possible through the Cross (Eph. 1:7; 1 Pet. 1:18-19).

Justification—the declaration or proclamation of a person as righteous, that is, possessing a right standing before God (Rom. 3:24).

Penal—God's punishing of Christ was the expression of God's judicial authority which demanded that sin must be paid for (Gal. 3:13).

Propitiation—Godward effect of the value of the cross; God is propitious in that Christ's sacrifice allowed God to execute His love and mercy for sinners without denying His justice, by fulfilling His judgment on the transgression against His will by sinful man (Rom. 1:18; 3:25-26; 4:15; 5:9; 1 Jn. 2:2; 4:10).

Reconciliation—Manward effect of the value of the Cross; the establishment of peace between God and man by the quenching of God's wrath and the changing of man's anti-God disposition (2 Cor. 5:16-21).

Redemption and Ransom—Christ's sacrifice provided a payment of a ransom price for the debt owed by man to God (2 Pet. 2:1; Rev. 5:9-10; 1 Cor. 6:19-20).

Satisfaction–God's acceptance of Christ's payment on the Cross (Acts 20:28).

Vicarious-the substitutionary effect of the Cross; i.e. in the place of sinners (Gal. 3:13; 4:5).

Medium of Salvation

In discussing the medium of salvation, the concern is identifying that process through which an unbeliever becomes a believer. The divine persons are not in view [e.g. we are saved by the Holy Spirit (1 Peter 1:2)], but rather those things used by the divine persons in order to accomplish their goal of salvation. There are several terms that are used to explain how one moves from darkness unto life. These terms are election, common grace, general call, effectual call, regeneration, faith, conversion, justification, sanctification, perseverance of the saints, and glorification. Each of these terms will be succinctly expounded.

Election
(Acts 13:44-48; Rom. 9:1-24; Eph. 1:3-6; 1 Pet. 1:1-2)

Election is that act of God whereby He sets aside by efficacious decree before the creation of the world a specific number from among the masses of hellbound men to be benefactors of His special act of salvation.

Common Grace
(Mt. 5:45; Jn. 16:5-11; Acts 14:15-18; 17:25; 2 Thess. 2:1-7)

Common grace is that working of the Holy Spirit in the world at large, which is short of regeneration, that restrains evil, allows for civil good, delays the judgment of God, convicts of sin, righteousness, and judgment, and through which God grants His kindness to mankind.

General Call
(Mt. 22:1-14; Rom. 10:1-21)

General call is that gracious invitation to receive the benefits of the salvation accomplished by Christ that is offered to all men, but although not always effectual, is still a genuine call. This call demonstrates God's righteous standard, and His love for sinners, and results in further condemnation for those who reject it, and salvation for those who accept it.

Effectual Call
(Jn. 6:35-44; Rom. 8:28-30)

The effectual call is that act of God whereby He definitively draws and regenerates those whom He has elected for salvation.

Regeneration
(Jn. 3:1-8; 2 Cor. 5:17; 1 Thess. 1:9-10; 1 Pet. 1:22-25)

Regeneration is that act of God whereby He changes the will of the sinner so that he now chooses that which he naturally resists, the good, and implants new life in him, with the result that he becomes a believer.

Faith
(Eph. 2:4-10)

Faith is that act of man whereby he claims for himself the new life and other benefits of Christ's atonement for himself, casting himself completely and wholly upon Christ for his eternal salvation, and it is a gift of God.

Conversion
(1 Thess. 1:9-10)

Conversion is that act of man whereby he turns from his own self-willed way of sin and embraces the Savior as his own.

Justification
(Rom. 3:21-5:21)

Justification is that act of God whereby he pronounces the regenerated sinner righteous in His sight. It is positional in nature.

Sanctification
(Rom. 6:1-8:39; Gal. 3:1-5; 5:1-25)

Sanctification is that act of God whereby He progressively makes the regenerated sinner righteous. This is a continual process while he is in a non-glorified state, and to which the believer responds with obedience and love of Christ, and this sanctification is positional, progressive, and prospective (future).

Perseverance
(Jn. 10:22-30; Rom. 8:28-30; Phil. 1:6; 2:12-13)

Perseverance of the saints is that continued act of the Holy Spirit in the believer's life whereby what God has begun in the believer's life is continued until the time of its completion, thereby assuring that none of God's elect are ultimately lost.

Glorification
(1 Cor. 15:1-58; 1 Jn. 3:1-3)

Glorification is that act of God whereby He resurrects or translates the believer from this earthly body into a heavenly body, made after the form of Christ.

This is the process whereby God brings about the salvation of man. It will be noticed that it begins in eternity past with God, is activated in the present through God, and is completed in the future by God. Salvation is a work of God, with which man has the joyous privilege of participating.

The Godhead and Salvation

Each member of the Trinity plays an intricate role in the believer's salvation. Rather than examining the multitude of passages on each person, we will examine just one of the many passages of Scripture that teach us the role each member of the Godhead plays, which is 1 Peter 1:2. It will be noticed here that our formula for the divine works—*of God, through the Son, unto the Father*—is still applicable.

The Father is the source or effectual cause of our salvation in that He chooses or foreknows us. The idea of foreknowing is not just prior knowledge of something, but is prior knowledge based on planning or predetermining something. This is manifested by Peter's combination of foreknowledge and the predetermined plan of God in Acts 2:22-23. To foreknow, then, refers to that counsel of God in which, after deliberative judgment, certain ones from mankind were chosen to a certain position, which is defined by the context in 1 Peter as salvation. What is the basis of this choosing? Just as in the case of Christ, it was all dependent upon God's choice and will, so it is here in 1 Peter 1:2. Therefore, Peter indicates to his readers that the basis of their election was God's foreordination. They were foreknown by God because they were foreordained by Him to be saved. It may be difficult to understand how one can have a prior relationship with someone who is still unborn, but there are two things that must be remembered about God. First, God is simple, and as such He knows all He knows all at once without sequence. Second, our adoption as believers is placed in eternity past with God. This of course means that

God had a relationship of Father/child with us before our historical birth took place. So God the Father is the originator of the plan.

The Holy Spirit is the immediate cause of our salvation in that He is the One who actually regenerates us. This verse speaks of the preparational sanctifying work of the Holy Spirit. This work of the Spirit sets the unbeliever apart from the realm of condemnation for the actual realm of salvation. So the work of the Spirit, in Peter's recipients being chosen, is that He is the One that marked or set them apart for something, which is defined by the context as salvation. Again we see the Holy Spirit at work in the life of believers as the most immediate or direct agent of action. It is interesting to note that the *making holy* of the believer ("sanctifying work") is done by the *Holy* Spirit. So, the Holy Spirit is the firsthand agent.

The Son, Jesus Christ our Savior, is that One who provides the means for our being saved. Thus, the purpose of them being foreordained by God and set apart by the Spirit, is in order that they may come to the point of placing faith in Jesus Christ. The act of faith brings on the sprinkling of the blood of Jesus Christ. The significance of this act of sprinkling is clearly illustrated with Moses, as well as the Levitical priesthood, when they sprinkled the people in order to cleanse them and, according to the Law, to forgive sin (Hebrews 9:11-22). Christ, the mediator of the new covenant, cleanses and forgives the sinner who comes to Him in faith. He provided the sacrifice that made salvation possible. He was the One who submitted Himself to the executioner's cross, in order to furnish the blood necessary to carry out the Father's plan, and supply the Spirit with the necessary blood with which to sprinkle us. So, the Son acts as the secondary agent.

APPLICATION

Salvation is the badge of valor which the believer wears. It simply reads "saved by grace." The believer's salvation is what summarizes who he is. If not for salvation it would be impossible for man to become a child of God. Of all the events in the believer's life, it is his salvation to which he is continually called. Time and time again he is pointed back to his salvation in order to spur him on to proper action in the present. It can be said that our salvation sets the temperature for our daily walk. Of the many important aspects of our salvation that we could apply to our spiritual growth, none are more important than our: 1) Abundant Thanksgiving; 2) Active Response; and 3) Appropriate Conduct. Each of these aspects to our salvation plays an important role in our spiritual life.

Our Abundant Thanksgiving
One of the most important responses to God that we can have is that of abundant thanksgiving for what God has done. The book of Romans serves as an excellent backdrop for understanding the spiritual ramifications of our salvation.

Paul's goal in its pages is to accurately and extensively expound the nature and results of justification/salvation. In doing this, Paul first demonstrates the condemnation of the whole human race and thus their need for justification (1:18-3:20). He then explains the process of justification by faith (3:21-5:21). Halfway through the book, Paul explains the outworking of justification, which is sanctification (6:1-8:39), followed by God's ability to carry out the promise of justification in His people (9:1-11:36). The last section of the book deals with the believer's practical response to God's work of justification in him (12:1-16:27). So it can be seen that justification/salvation is the issue of this book.

One of the most important sections on salvation found in this book is Romans 9:1-24. In this chapter Paul deals with the doctrine of election and its relationship to the believer's attitude towards God. Paul first explains that election is a choice between people, and is not based on their works whether good or evil (9:1-13). He then explains that election is a choice of God to show mercy to a person that is determined and applied regardless of a person's will or effort (9:14-18). At the end of this last section, Paul makes a comment that we will do well to understand. God's purpose in carrying out salvation in this way was to ensure that the maximum amount of glory went to Himself (9:23). God Himself states that He is a jealous God (Exodus 20:5), meaning that He refuses to share His glory with anyone. Since salvation depends entirely upon God, He gets all of the glory for it. Through this act, He made known to us the sheer magnitude of His richness in glory. In other words the purpose for accomplishing salvation by the means that He accomplished it was to communicate to each individual believer His great amount of love to them. To this we should give abundant thanksgiving for all that He has done on our behalf. Paul puts it this way,

> "But God **demonstrates** His own **love toward us**, in that while we were yet sinners, **Christ died for us**. Much more then, having now been justified by His blood, we shall be **saved from the wrath of God** through Him. For if while we were enemies, we were **reconciled to God** through the death of His Son, much more, having been reconciled, we shall be **saved by His life**. And not only this, but **we** also **exult** in God through our Lord Jesus Christ, through whom we have now received the reconciliation" (Rom. 5:8-11) (emphasis added).

It is clear that the natural response to what God has supernaturally done for the believer is that of exulting Him. A saved Christian is one who is a thankful Christian, thankful for what his Lord has done for him.

Our Active Response
Christianity is a belief system that is built on action. The believer should be doing the will of His Savior, both in his

service and his obedience. Another key passage in the book of Romans is Romans 12:1-2. These two verses function as transitional verses from the doctrinal section of Romans (1-11) to the practical section of Romans (12-16). These verses are a bridge. Paul opens up the verse by saying, "I urge you therefore, brethren, by the mercies of God . . ." This opening statement sums up the first eleven chapters. Because of the mercies of God expressed in salvation, we should respond in a certain way. This response is not speaking to the issue of our praise as did the first section, but rather our practice.

The response is two-fold: 1) presenting (12:1); and 2) conforming (12:2). We should respond with the presentation of our bodies to God. Our bodies should be presented "living and holy", that is, consumed with a spiritually active godly life. The second aspect to the believer's response is that of transformation. By transformation we mean the process in the believer's life in which he resists the conforming power of the world, by the ongoing interaction with the Word of God which spurs the renewal of his thinking process, with the result that he conforms himself to the will of God. This process or practice, which Paul calls the believer's "spiritual service of worship," will result in his approving the "good and acceptable and perfect *will of God*" (italics added). Our active response is thus to present ourselves to God and conform ourselves to His will.

Our Appropriate Conduct

As believers we realize that there is much to which we are responsible. One of the more significant passages in this regard is that which is found in Ephesians chapter two. This passage expounds on the nature of our salvation (2:1-10), as well as the result of our salvation as it deals with the body of Christ, that is, the church (2:11-22). An important statement is found in Ephesians 2:10, and it says, "For we are His workmanship, created in Christ Jesus for good works, which God prepared beforehand, that we should walk in them." This is an interesting verse because it tells the believer exactly why he has the responsibility that was given him, what his responsibility is, as well as when it is to start.

The believer's responsibility is the way it is because of the fact that his salvation is the way it is. It will be noticed that this verse begins with the word "for" which tells the reader that Paul is giving the reason or basis for his preceding comments. The nature of the believer's responsibility is tied to the nature of his salvation. This same link is made other places in Paul's writings (Gal. 3:1-3). So what is the believer's responsibility that is founded upon his salvation? Our responsibility is found in God's purpose for recreating us. That purpose is "for good works." God saved us in order that we might pursue good works. These good works, according to the passage, are works that God has prepared for us to participate in. This is instructive because we learn that living a life of holiness is what God has planned from eternity past for us. When God chose us, He also determined the good works He desired for us to do. Thus, while we are not saved by good works (Eph 2:9), we are saved for good works. Where is the believer to find these good works in which he is supposed to walk? The source of these good works is the Word of God from which we discover all that God wants us to do and be (cf. 2 Tim. 3:16-17). If, in fact, our salvation is by faith, our sanctification must be by faith as well.

Chapter Nine
THE HOLY SPIRIT

"I. The Holy Spirit as the bond that unites us to Christ

We must now examine this question. How do we receive those benefits which the Father bestowed on his only-begotten Son — not for Christ's own private use, but that he might enrich poor and needy men? First, we must understand that as long as Christ remains outside of us, and we are separated from him, all that he has suffered and done for the salvation of the human race remains useless and of no value for us. Therefore, to share with us what he has received from the Father, he had to become ours and to dwell within us. For this reason, he is called "our Head" [Eph. 4:15], and "the first-born among many brethren" [Rom. 8:29]. We also, in turn, are said to be "engrafted into him" [Rom. 11:17], and to "put on Christ" [Gal. 3:27]; for, as I have said, all that he possesses is nothing to us until we grow into one body with him. It is true that we obtain this by faith. Yet since we see that not all indiscriminately embrace that communion with Christ which is offered through the gospel, reason itself teaches us to climb higher and to examine into the secret energy of the Spirit, by which we come to enjoy Christ and all his benefits.

Earlier I discussed the eternal deity and essence of the Spirit. Now let us be content with this particular point: that Christ so "came by water and blood" in order that the Spirit may witness concerning him [I John 5:6-7], lest the salvation imparted through him escape us. For, as three witnesses in heaven are named — the Father, the Word, and the Spirit — so there are three on earth: the water, the blood, and the Spirit [I John 5:7-8]. There is good reason for the repeated mention of the "testimony of the Spirit," a testimony we feel engraved like a seal upon our hearts, with the result that it seals the cleansing and sacrifice of Christ. For this reason, also, Peter says that believers have been "chosen in the sanctification of the Spirit unto obedience and sprinkling of the blood of Christ" [I Peter 1:2 p.]. By these words he explains that, in order that the shedding of his sacred blood may not be nullified, our souls are cleansed by the secret watering of the Spirit. For the same reason, also, Paul, in speaking of cleansing and justification, says that we come to possess both, "in the name of ... Jesus Christ and in the Spirit of our God" [I Cor. 6:11]. To sum up, the Holy Spirit is the bond by which Christ effectually unites us to himself. To this, also, pertains what we taught in the previous book concerning his anointing."[24]

DOCTRINE

The study of the Holy Spirit is important to any exposition or explanation of Christian doctrine. As part of the Trinity the Holy Spirit is a central aspect to the Christian faith. Studying Him is also very important in that we have many people today who have adopted a skewed perspective on the nature and work of the Holy Spirit, and as such a clearer interpretation is needed for our time that will speak to these issues. Our study will primarily focus on three aspects relative to the Holy Spirit, which are: 1) the Deity of the Spirit; 2) the Person of the Spirit; and 3) the Ministries of the Spirit.

The Deity of the Spirit

Of importance here is whether or not the Holy Spirit is actually God. Can it be said of Him that He is deity? Or rather, why do we say that the Holy Spirit is deity? There are three major lines of evidence which demonstrate the deity of the Spirit, they are: 1) His attributes; 2) His actions; and 3) His names.

The Holy Spirit exhibits attributes that are possessed only by God, which, therefore, must indicate that He is God. The Spirit is eternal (Heb. 9:14), omnipotent (Compare Eph. 1:18-20 with 1 Pet. 3:18–the surpassing power of the resurrection which God has also attributed to the Holy Spirit), omnipresent (Ps. 139:7-10), omniscient (1 Cor. 2:10-11), loving (Gal. 5:22), true (1 Jn. 5:6), and holy ("the Holy Spirit").

Many of the things or works that the Holy Spirit does are divine works. In other words, they are acts which are attributed to God. They are as follows: 1) creation (Gen. 1:2; Ps. 104:30); 2) inspiration (compare 2 Tim. 3:16 with 2 Pet. 1:20-21); 3) generation of Christ (Lk. 1:35); 4) regeneration (Tit. 3:5; Jn. 1:12-13; 3:3-5); and 5) illumination (1 Cor. 2:6-

13). This is a short list of divine works which are attributed to the Spirit. Another strong proof of the Holy Spirit's deity is that His name is invoked at the believer's baptism. Believers are baptized in the name of the Father and the Son and the Holy Spirit (Mt. 28:19).

Several titles are given to the Holy Spirit which indicate that He is deity. As well as being called the Holy Spirit or the Spirit, He is also called the Spirit of God (1 Cor. 2:11; 1 Pet. 4:14), the Spirit of Christ (Gal. 4:6; Rom. 8:9; Phil. 1:19; 1 Pet. 1:11), "another Helper" (Jn. 14:16–which in the Greek means another of the same kind), and the One who precedes from the Father and Christ (Jn. 14:16, 26; 15:26; 16:7).

The Person of the Spirit

The personality of the Holy Spirit is clearly demonstrated in the Scriptures and can be proven on several different levels. There are three types of proofs of His personality.

First, the Holy Spirit both possesses and expresses the attributes of personality. As noted in anthropology, personhood consists of intellect, emotions, will, and dominion. It is clear that the Holy Spirit has intellect from the fact that He knows and searches the deep things of God (1 Cor. 2:10-11), possesses a mind (Rom. 8:27), and teaches believers (Jn. 14:26; 1 Cor. 2:13). It is clear that He expresses emotion from the fact that He may be grieved (Eph. 4:30). Second, the evidence is also clear that the Holy Spirit has a will by the fact that He uses such in distributing gifts to believers (1 Cor. 12:11), and He accomplishes what He wills in others and guides their activities (Ac. 16:6-11; Jn. 14:17, 26; 15:26). Finally, the evidence is also clear that He has dominion by the fact that He is the creator of the world (Gen. 1:2; cf. Job 26:13; and Ps. 33:6).

The Holy Spirit acts in ways only a person could act. He teaches (Jn. 14:26), testifies (Jn. 15:26), guides into truth (Jn. 16:13), speaks (Jn. 16:13), convicts (Jn. 16:8), helps and intercedes (Rom. 8:26), and works miracles (Ac. 8:39).

The Holy Spirit is acted upon in only ways that a person could be acted upon. He can be blasphemed (Mt. 12:31), grieved (Eph. 4:30), insulted (He. 10:29), lied to (Ac. 5:3), and resisted (Ac. 7:51).

Lastly, the Spirit receives certain ascriptions which indicate that He must be a person. First, He is viewed as One among persons (Ac. 15:28—". . . to the Holy Spirit and to us (the apostles) . . ."; cf. Ac. 5:1-16—Ananias thought himself to be lying to man, but He was actually lying to the Holy Spirit). Second, He is of the same character as Jesus Christ, who was also a person (Jn. 14:16). Third, He is referred to with the Greek masculine pronoun of "He" (Jn. 16:13-14).

The Ministries of the Spirit

The ministries of the Holy Spirit may be easily divided into two sections. His ministries are: 1) in the Old Testament and 2) in the New Testament.

The Spirit in the Old Testament

Creation: The Spirit was involved in creation (see above verses). **Communication:** The Holy Spirit was involved in revelation and inspiration. Specific verses indicate that the prophets spoke by means of the Holy Spirit (2 Sam. 23:2; Mic. 3:8). The New Testament authors also attribute the Old Testament to the Holy Spirit (Mt. 22:43; Ac. 4:25; 28:25; 2 Pet. 1:21). **Community:** As to His work in people during the Old Testament, there is a marked difference from the New Testament. Jesus made it clear and emphasized that the Holy Spirit was coming. This indicated that what Jesus was referring to was a different type of presence than what the Holy Spirit was involved with in the Old Testament. This must be the case because the Holy Spirit was clearly active in the Old Testament, so His coming must refer to what He was to do once He came. **Contrasts:** While the Spirit is in all New Testament (NT) believers, only a few in the Old Testament (OT) are said to have the Spirit in them (Gen. 41:38; Num. 27:18; Dan. 4:8; 5:11-14; 6:3). While the Spirit comes upon all NT believers, only a few in the OT are said to have the Spirit come upon them (Num. 24:2; Jdgs. 3:10; 6:34; 11:29, etc.). Such seems to occur to help in one specific event and is not continued after that event is over. While all NT believers are commanded to be filled with the Holy Spirit, only twice are OT people said to be filled with the Holy Spirit (Ex. 31:3; 35:31). Again such occurs only for a specific event. **Conclusion:** It may be said that the ministry of the Holy Spirit in the Old Testament was limited in its scope. It was limited as to the people He was involved with, and the type of ministry to those people that He had, as well as the length of such ministries to those people.

The Spirit in the New Testament
The ministries of the Holy Spirit in the New Testament are very numerous. What follows is a concise list of each.

Indwelling: The indwelling of the Holy Spirit is the act of the Holy Spirit at the moment of conversion whereby He permanently abides or dwells in the believer in such a way that the believer is now once again God's property (Rom. 8:9; 1 Cor. 3:16; 6:19).

Sealing: The sealing is that act of the Holy Spirit at the time of conversion whereby He secures the believer's future inheritance, both assuring him of his eternal position in Christ and granting to him the spiritual down payment of such (2 Cor. 1:22; Eph. 1:13; Eph. 4:30).

Baptism: Baptism is that act of the Holy Spirit at the time of conversion whereby He places the believer in the body of Christ, the church, the bride of Christ; paralleling the death, burial, and resurrection of Christ (1 Cor. 12:13; Eph. 4).

Gifting: Gifting is that act of the Holy Spirit at the time of conversion and on an ongoing basis whereby He equips the believer with a special ability in a particular area of exhortation for the body of Jesus Christ (1 Cor. 12; Rom. 12; Eph. 4).

Filling: The filling is that act of the Holy Spirit after conversion whereby He controls the actions and desires of the believer who is yielded to His influence (Eph. 5:18).

Teaching: Teaching is that act of the Holy Spirit after conversion whereby He instructs the believer through the Word, both to its general meaning and application (Jn. 16:12-15).

Guiding: Guiding is that act of the Holy Spirit after conversion whereby He leads and directs the believer in his decisions, choices, and actions; paralleling the filling of the Holy Spirit (Rom. 8:14).

Assuring: Assuring is that act of the Holy Spirit after conversion whereby He confirms and reassures the believer in his inner man that he is a child of God (Rom. 8:16).

Praying: Praying is that act of the Holy Spirit after conversion whereby He understands, interprets, translates, and communicates to God, the believer's non-understandable and incommunicable needs, perplexities, and problems during times of prayer and supplication (Rom. 8:26).

APPLICATION

More than any other member of the Trinity, the Bible places emphasis on the Spirit as the Divine Enabler. In theology there is a formula that is used to distinguish the differing functions of the members of the Trinity. This formula helps us understand the precise nature of the Spirit's role. In studying the Trinity we learned that works of God are **of** the Father, **through** the Son, **by** the Spirit, and **Unto** the Father. The Spirit is the immediate agent in the things that the Trinity does, which is everything. With this in mind there are three important elements of the Spirit's enablement for the Christian's growth, which are: 1) the Spirit as the Controller; 2) the Spirit as the Indweller; and 3) the Spirit as the Engifter. Each of these functions of the Holy Spirit plays an important role in the believer's life.

The Spirit as the Controller

The Spirit's function as Controller of the believer's life refers to what the Bible calls filling. The major passage in this regard is found in Ephesians 5:15-21. In the eighteenth verse of this section Paul says, "And do not get drunk with wine, for that is dissipation, but be filled with the Spirit." This imperative falls in a section full of imperatives (5:15-21) and stands on its own. Paul compares being filled with the Spirit, as the same as getting drunk with wine. Paul makes it clear that he is making a contrast between getting drunk and being filled by the Spirit (notice the use of "but"). The difficult part in understanding this passage is understanding the nature of the contrast. Is being filled with the Spirit opposite in effect or opposite in action? The answer is really both.

Being filled with the Spirit produces opposite effects to getting drunk. Rather than being out of control (influenced by wine), you are under control (influenced by God). Being filled with the Spirit is also opposite in action. That is, it is the godly opposite to being drunk. Both the influence of wine and the influence of God, have to do with control. When one is filled with wine he is no longer in control of himself, and when one is filled with God he is also no longer in control of himself. Both deal with control, but from different perspectives. One leads to recklessness ("for that is dissipation") and one leads to submissiveness (5:19-20). While this passage indicates the fact of filling, the method of filling is found in Colossians 3:16.

In this passage Paul commands his readers to let "the word of Christ richly dwell within you." The way that the Christian knows these two ideas are parallel is that both the filling of the Spirit and the Word of Christ richly dwelling produce the same results of edifying one another, worshiping in one's heart, and giving thanks to God in Christ's name (compare Eph. 5:18-21 and Col. 3:16-17). It will also be noticed that both passages are followed by exhortation to family members, slaves, and masters (Eph. 5:22-6:9; Col. 3:18-4:6). Therefore, the filling of the Spirit is really allowing the Word of God to abundantly take up residence in your life. Therefore, the believer who wants to be controlled by the Holy Spirit, must be controlled by the Word of God.

The Spirit as the Indweller

When Jesus left the earth, He promised the disciples another Helper. This was a reference to the Spirit that would dwell in all believers. The indwelling Spirit functions in a multiplicity of ways in the believer's life. Although several of these functions are of great significance to spiritual growth, we will make mention of just a few. One important function of the Indwelling Spirit is that of being the basis of our holiness. In 1 Corinthians 3:16 Paul says, "Do you not know that you are a temple of God, and that the Spirit of God dwells in you?" The Holy Spirit also directs the believer to God. Galatians 4:6 affirms, "And because you are sons, God has sent forth the Spirit of His Son into our hearts, crying, Abba! Father!" The Holy Spirit is also the foundation of the believers' assurance. 1 John 4:13 says, "By this we know that we abide in Him and He in us, because He has given us of His Spirit" (cf. Rom. 8:16). If the Spirit indwells the believer's life, then he has the responsibility to live in light of that indwelling.

The Spirit as the Engifter

As noted in the doctrinal section of our discussion, the Holy Spirit is the One who gifts the believer. Each believer, at the time of his conversion, is given a spiritual gift that is given for the edification of the body of Jesus Christ. Probably one of the clearest passages on the gifts of the Holy Spirit is found in 1 Corinthians 12. In 1 Corinthians 12:4-7, Paul instructs that the Spirit engifts believers for the edification of the other believers in the body. Verse seven says, "But to each one is given the manifestation of the Spirit for the common good." The exercise of the gifts is an important aspect to growth. The church of Jesus Christ is likened to a body (1 Cor. 12:27).

For a body to function properly, each member or part of the body must function appropriately. As in any human body, for the body of Christ to function properly, each member of the body of Christ must also function appropriately and use its gift properly. When one member decides it is not going to function as it is supposed to, that renegade member causes the rest of the body to malfunction. So if I, as a member of the body of Christ, decide that I am not going to exercise my spiritual gift, then I cause the malfunction of the body of Christ, and in turn, affect my own growth because of it. When the body is not growing properly, I am adversely affected (1 Cor. 12:22-26).[25]

Part Four

◆

God's Summation

The Church and the End Times
and Their Implications for Spiritual Growth

Chapter Ten
THE CHURCH

"I. The catholic or universal Church, which is invisible, consists of the whole number of the elect, that have been, are, or shall be gathered into one, under Christ the head thereof; and is the spouse, the body, the fullness of him that filleth all in all.

II. The visible Church, which is also catholic or universal under the gospel (not confined to one nation as before under the law) consists of all those, throughout the world, that profess the true religion, and of their children; and is the kingdom of the Lord Jesus Christ, the house and family of God, out of which there is no ordinary possibility of salvation.

III. Unto this catholic visible Church Christ hath given the ministry, oracles, and ordinances of God, for the gathering and perfecting of the saints, in this life, to the end of the world: and doth by his own presence and Spirit, according to his promise, make them effectual thereunto.

IV. This catholic Church hath been sometimes more, sometimes less visible. And particular churches, which are members thereof, are more or less pure, according as the doctrine of the gospel is taught and embraced, ordinances administered, and public worship performed more or less purely in them.

V. The purest churches under heaven are subject both to mixture and error; and some have so degenerated as to become no churches of Christ, but synagogues of Satan. Nevertheless, there shall always be a Church on earth to worship God according to his will."[26]

DOCTRINE

There can be little doubt that one of God's major works in human history is that of the church of Jesus Christ. Almost the entire New Testament is given over to its explanation and description, and much of the Old Testament is used for its proof and its teachings. Our study of the church will encompass five areas: 1) The Church as to its Nature; 2) The Church as to its Relationship to the Program of God; 3) The Church as to its Government; 4) The Church as to its Membership; and 5) The Church as to its Ordinances.

The Nature of the Church

In looking at the nature of the church, one is immediately presented with a great difficulty. Because the church is a multifaceted organism, trying to concisely describe it is arduous to say the least. Such a presentation, however, can be adequately accomplished through an analysis of the universal church, the local church, and the images of the church used in the Bible.

The universal church is that whole body of persons from Pentecost through to the rapture who have been savingly reconciled to God through Christ's death and resurrection, and thus received new life. It is composed of both those who are in heaven and on the earth, and is invisible in its nature, meaning there is not one central location during the church age to which the universal church may be located (1 Cor. 10:32; 11:22; 12:28; Eph. 4:11-16).

The local church is a particular local manifestation of the universal church. It is not different from the universal church, but rather displays the same qualities as does the body of Christ as a whole (1 Cor. 11:18; 14:19, 28, 35; 16:1; Rom. 16:4; Gal. 1:2; 1 Thess. 2:14). There are four marks which distinguish the presence of a local body of believers.

The Word

First, the preaching and teaching of the Word is carried out in order to increase faith and obedience (1 Tim. 3:14-15; 4:6; 2 Tim. 4:1-5; Tit. 1:9; Jude 3).

The Sacraments

Second, the administration of the Sacraments is carried out in order to confirm faith and obedience (Lk. 22:14-23; 1 Cor. 1:13-17; 11:23-34).

Discipline

Third, ecclesiastical discipline is carried out in order to censure vices contrary to faith and obedience (Matt. 18:15-20; 1 Cor. 5:1-13).

Inner Relationship

Fourth, the church exhibits both unity and diversity. Diversity in spiritual maturity, gifts, and ultimate glory. Unity in reference to the object of their faith, message, and covenant (Eph. 2:1-4:16).

The Images of the Church

There are six basic images which are used in the New Testament to illustrate the nature of the church. What follows is the list of such with a concise definition.

The Body of Christ

The Body of Christ speaks to the church in its universal character, meaning all believers make up the body of Christ. The major ideas being conveyed through this metaphor are unity, diversity, mutuality, leadership (head down), source, and sustenance (1 Cor. 12:12-31; Rom. 12:5; Eph. 1:22-23; 4:4, 12, 16; 5:30; Col. 1:18, 24; 2:19).

The Temple of God

The Temple of God speaks to the church being the dwelling place of God, the place in which He takes up habitation. Also being conveyed is the idea of holiness (purity), ownership, and dedication (separateness) (Eph. 2:19-22; cf. 1 Cor. 3:10-11; 1 Pet. 2:4-8).

The Priesthood

The Priesthood, which is the corollary to the Temple, speaks to the individual member specifically. That which is being conveyed here are the ideas of chosen and separateness of the individual believers, and the functions of sacrifice for intercession, service, and access to God (1 Pet. 2:9).

The Bride of Christ

The Bride of Christ speaks to the unique relationship between the church and Christ. The ideas being conveyed here are love, responsiveness, and future union of the bride and bridegroom (Jn. 3:29; Rom. 7:4; 2 Cor. 11:2; Rev. 21:2, 9).

The Flock of God

The Flock of God speaks to the issue of the dependency and submissiveness of the church, emphasizing how it relates to its leadership. The ideas being conveyed are that of the shepherding of the flock (leadership, local usually), ownership of the flock by God, and the subjection of the flock (Jn. 10:11-30; 21:16; Eph. 4:11; 1 Pet. 5:2).

The Vine and the Branches

The Vine and the Branches speak to the issue of fruitfulness and its source. The ideas conveyed here are that of the organic union of the vine and the branches, the necessity of fruitfulness, the source of fruitfulness, and the method of fruitfulness (John 15:1-11).

The Relationship of the Church to God's Kingdom Program

In discussing the church in the program of God there are several important distinctions which must be made. Two of the more important ones will be discussed at this time: 1) the relationship of the church to the kingdom; and 2) the relationship of the church to Israel.

From the creation of Adam, God's desire for the human race has been the establishing of His kingdom on the earth. We know this from the summing up of human history in Revelation 20 with the kingdom of Christ on the earth. Such a kingdom would be an imploding of the universal kingdom of God in time and space on the earth. A kingdom is made up of a ruler, a realm, and a ruled. Each element is needed for the existence of a kingdom. When man continually rejected God's purposes in this regard (Gen.1-11), God narrowed His focus to one man, who would eventually make up one nation. He established with that man and his offspring several covenants that would assure that a mediatorial (a kingdom of God ruled by a vice regent) kingdom would eventually be setup on the earth. The man was Abraham and the nation would be Israel. Israel's rejection of her Messiah, God's ultimate viceroy, meant that humanly speaking His plans for them needed to be postponed, but in the interim, God established the spiritual aspects of the kingdom promises with an entirely new entity called the church (Eph. 2:15). This present age, the church age, will end with Christ's second coming, at which time, the times of the Gentiles will be over, and God will once again resume His concentrated work on and in Israel (Rom. 9-11).

The relationship of the church and Israel may be simply put as being distinct from it, yet related to it. They are distinct in that the church is not Israel, but rather a new organism. It does not receive the covenants of God nor does it supplant Israel in the program of God (Rom. 9-11; Eph. 2). They are related in that the church and Israel are both peoples of God, share in the covenant (Israel as the receivers, the church as benefactors), and have the same Lord (the church now, Israel later). These are just a few of the distinctives and relationships, but many more could be stated.

The Government of the Church

Probably one of the areas of greatest difference in the organization and construction of a local church is that of church government. These forms vary from very loose associations to very complex systems of organization with multi-level checks and balances. The flexibility afforded this area in Scripture must of course be brought under the control of the Holy Spirit, the moving force behind the church, and the models provided by the Scriptures. We will look at the background of church government, as well as the types of church government that have developed throughout church history.

The early church evidenced characteristics which indicated that they possessed some type of church organization. This is clear because: 1) they exhibited doctoral conformity, that is, their beliefs were the same (Ac. 2:42); 2) they baptized (Ac. 2:41); 3) they participated in the Lord's Supper (Ac. 2:42, 46); 4) they tracked membership (Ac. 2:14, 41; 4:4); 5) they helped those in need (Ac. 2:44, 45); and 6) they appointed leaders (Ac. 6:1-7).

It should also be noted that they had: 1) church officers (Ac. 14:23; 1 Tim. 3:1-13; Tit. 1:5; 1 Pe. 5:1-4); 2) stated gatherings on the first day of the week (Jn. 20:19, 26; Ac. 20:7; 1 Cor. 16:2; Rev. 1:10); 3) church discipline (Mt. 18:15-20; 1 Cor. 5:13); and 4) raised financial support for the needy (1 Cor. 16:1-2; 2 Cor. 9:6-7).

While it might be a partially true statement that there are as many forms of church government as there are local churches, most churches fit into one of five categories. Some churches may use a hybrid form of two or more types of church government, but creation of a whole new form is unlikely.

Episcopalian

The episcopalian form of church government maintains a three-fold ministry of the church: bishops, presbyters (priest), and deacons. The bishop is the only one with the right to consecrate other bishops and ordain priests and deacons. This calls for a different degree or level of ordination. The clergy below the deacon can perform all the basic duties such as preach and administer the sacraments. Beyond this is the special powers vested in the bishop.

Presbyterian

The presbyterian church government operates on rulership by elders as representatives of the church. Each church is resided over by the ruling elders (chosen by the membership) and the teaching elder or minister as the presiding officer. Next is the presbytery which is composed of all the teaching elders and one ruling elder from each church in a given district. Over the presbytery is the synod and over it is the general assembly. Both of these, the presbytery and the synod, are divided between teaching elders and ruling elders. The presbyters choose both the members of the synod and the general assembly. Both teaching and ruling (laymen) elders are on parity, however the ruling elders govern the church, while the teaching elder ministers the Word and sacraments. Appeals must work up a chain. Only teaching elders attend the general assembly.

Congregational

The congregational form of church government rests on the authority of each local church as an autonomous unit. There is no person or organization over the local church. The minister or officers have no more ecclesiastical authority than other members. Everybody has one vote on any issue. The officers vary in a church. There may be a plurality of elders who give the general oversight, and deacons who serve, or a pastor and deacons, with the deacons also being concerned with oversight. Ordination does not give a special status to the one ordained, for any laymen could do the same if so called by God. Each local church calls its own pastor and sets its own budget. The highest court of appeal is the local church. Doctrinal stability rests in the local church.

Erastian

The erastian form of church government holds that the church is simply a society owing its existence from two regulations enacted by the state. While the officers of the church are instructors or preachers of the Word, they have no power or right of rule independent of the civil magistrates. The state is to govern the church, conducting discipline and excommunication. Any such discipline is civil punishment, although carried out by the officers of the church. The extent of the relationship between the state and the national church may vary, but there is always some tie.

Minimalistic

The minimalist form of church government holds that all forms of external church formation are to be rejected. In their opinion any such church government is contrary to the spirit of Christianity and is sinful, for it exalts the human and subjugates the divine.

The Essentials of Church Membership

One of the most significant elements in the proper functioning of a local church is the implementation of membership, as well as the practice of the sacraments or ordinances of the church. The issue of membership has become even more acute today with the proliferation of churches and denominations. It is thus important to know the basis of such.

Are Christians responsible to be church members? Although membership is not mentioned in the New Testament, there are several principles that indicate that church membership is important for believers.

While some do not believe that membership is important or even required in the church, there are three good reasons for its existence. As to church membership, the New Testament knows nothing of a Christian who does not attend church and is joined in such a way to that church so as he could be considered a participating component of the larger group (Heb. 10:23-25). Without membership, accountability is impossible as is the practice of spiritual edification and the practice of the gifts (1 Cor. 5:1-13; Gal. 6:1-6; Heb. 10:23-25; 13:17). The local church is the God ordained means for care for the believer's growth, ministry to and from (practice of the gifts), and for the believer to demonstrate his commitment to Christ (1 Cor. 12:1-14:40; Heb. 13:17; 1 Peter 5:1-4; 1 Jn. 2:18-19).

Since church membership is not directly spoken of in the New Testament, qualifications for such will have to be gleaned from the requirements spoken of for being part of God's called out community, the *ecclesia*, Greek for church.

As to the qualifications for church membership the first and foremost is the regeneration of the individual seeking such. If one cannot belong to Christ without regeneration, neither can he be part of His church body (1 Cor. 12:12-14; Eph. 2:1-22). Next a certain level of comprehension is required, evidenced by confession, the understanding of the essentials of the gospel, as well as the profession of its reception, resulting in regeneration, the first requisite (Heb. 3:1; 4:14; 10:23). It is also necessary for the one seeking membership to be baptized. Baptism is the symbol of the spiritual transaction which united the person with Christ in the saving events of the death and resurrection of Christ (Mt. 28:18-20; Rom. 6:3-7).

The Ordinances of the Church

The ordinances of the church focus on the ritualistic observances practiced by the church that were instituted by Jesus Christ while He ministered on the earth. These observances portray a particular aspect of the church's relationship to Christ.

Our focus here will be the nature of an ordinance, or what makes an ordinance an ordinance. There are three elements that signify the presence of an ordinance: 1) it is accompanied by a command to participate in it; 2) it represents the relationship of Christ to His church, focusing particularly upon His death; and 3) it is witnessed to in the practice of the early church. The two ordinances which contain these three elements are Baptism and the Lord's Table.

The meaning of baptism is identification with Christ. It is an act of association or identification with someone, some group, some message, or some event. Therefore, first and foremost, it is identification with Christ. By this act, the initiate or new convert, indicates that he is entering the realm of the lordship and power of Jesus Christ. At this time he confesses his submission to the lordship of Christ in repentance and faith (Ac. 22:16; Rom. 10:9). It thus evidences the working of the gospel through which the believer is united to God. This process is done through Christ by God Himself, and the believer testifies to such a union in his life. It is a visible sign and seal of an inward and invisible event (regeneration), whereof God works in us by the power of the Holy Spirit. As such, it also serves as initiation into the church. It also pictures the believer's baptism by the Holy Spirit (Rom. 6:3-4).

Both by command and example, the Scriptures testify to the importance of baptism. First, baptism is included in the Great Commission, although not a part of the gospel itself. The disciples were told to go out into the whole world and make disciples. This would include preaching the gospel, people committing themselves to such through faith in Christ, and after such a time, being baptized in the name of the triune God, afterwhich they were to be taught everything Jesus said. Baptism was to be a sign and seal of the fact that they entered into a new relationship with God, and thus to live in light of that new relationship (Mt. 28:19-20). To not follow through on Christ's command and example in this facet is to be disobedient to His instruction.

The Lord's Table is that act of the local church inaugurated by Christ at the last supper with the disciples including bread and wine, which is pronounced as His body and His blood (Mt. 26:26-29; Mk. 14:22-25; Lk. 22:17-20; 1 Cor. 11:23-32). The elements represent the promise of grace attached to them. The bread represents His body given for the believer, and only does when it is related to that promise, otherwise all bread would represent His body, which would be quite absurd. The same holds true for the wine. It represents His blood, which was shed to atone for the believer's sin. It is said to be the seal to the truthfulness or fact of the promise. Because of the relationship of faith to the word and to the promise, once the sacraments, being administered rightly, are received through faith, the recipient receives assurance of God's fulfillment of such promises within that particular believer. As such, they are a means of assurance, which is needed for spiritual growth. The elements would be nothing without the word, but an empty exercise. Without the word there is no sacrament. If there is no promise (word) to accompany the sacrament, then it affords us nothing.

APPLICATION

In a very real sense, the study of the church is the corporate corollary to the study of salvation. The latter deals with individual salvation, while the former deals with corporate salvation. God is not just in the business of perfecting individual believers, He is also concerned with the perfection of His church. The Bible recognizes both the individual and corporate nature of the church and presents its truth for both individual and corporate consumption. God has so made man that he does not grow or mature in a vacuum. It is through relationships that people grow, both physically and spiritually. In spite of the heartache some relationships can cause in the lives of believers, it is only through relationships that one is able to find completion or growth in his Christian walk. As such, it is important for us to take note of the truth the Bible presents in reference to the Christian's relationship to a local body. There are a multiplicity of teachings in this regard that are important to the believer, that reference his spiritual growth, but we will look at only three. They are: 1) The Fruit of Fellowship; 2) The Significance of Service; and 3) The Mandate to the Ministry. Each of these aspects to our salvation play an important role in our spiritual life.

The Fruit of Fellowship

The Fruit of Fellowship speaks to the benefit derived by the believer from the fellowship of the saints in his life. In other words, what happens when Christians fellowship with each other? A good passage in this regard is that which is found in Hebrews 10:24-25. This passage comes at the end of an important sequence in the book of Hebrews, in which the author is attempting to close out a rather lengthy discussion on the benefits of Christ's sacrifice on behalf of man. In this section the author gives one of the responses the believer should have regarding Christ's provision of an access to God and Christ's ministry as our priest before God (Heb. 10:19-21; for the first two responses see 10:22). Our response according to this passage should be the stimulation of one another. The purpose of this stimulation is for the accomplishment of two things: 1) so that we would be better lovers and 2) better doers of His Word.

Love is the *sine qua non* of the Christian life (Jn. 13:35), and good deeds are the God ordained purpose of the Christian life (Eph. 2:10). It is interesting to note the author's use of the word that has been translated "stimulate" (or "spur" in some translations). This term in the Greek literally means to *irritate or exasperate.* As can be seen, this word is usually used in a negative sense. The fact that in this context it is used in a positive sense is quite peculiar. The author of Hebrews realized that many times it is going to take difficulties in relationships in order to produce growth. Another helpful way to understand this use of the word here is that of a coach inciting his team to a winning response. It is pushing another person to growth.

The author of Hebrews does not stop there, however, he goes on to tell his readers how this is done. In 10:25 he says, "not forsaking our own assembling together . . . but encouraging one another." It is through the gathering of believers together in local assemblies for the purpose of mutual encouragement that this stimulating effect is produced. When we relate to others in the intimate relationship of brother and sister in Christ, stimulation occurs, we are compelled to relate to others properly, thus causing a spiritual chafing effect that is to produce spiritual growth. This is the fruit of fellowship. If we want to grow spiritually we must be faithful in our attendance and participation in a local body of believers.

The Significance of Service

The significance of service focuses on the importance of service to the believer's spiritual growth. It is important to realize that the Christian life is as much giving as it is receiving. This is plainly indicated in Ephesians 4:16. Coming to the end of one of the more important points in this epistle, Ephesians 4:16 teaches us the importance of every believer joining in the spiritual growth process.

This section begins in 4:11-13 with a statement as to the role of the church leaders in the growth process of laymen. It is their responsibility, according to this passage, to equip the laymen in their charge to do ministry, to do the "work of service," Paul says. In doing so, the laymen build up the body of Christ to the point of each member of that particular local body reaching the full maturity expected of them in Christ. We do not learn how this takes place until 4:16. When each person does the "work of service" spoken of in 4:12, they are supplying something to the body. Ephesians 4:16 says it this way, "from whom the whole body, being fitted and held together by that which every joint supplies . . ." Paul goes on in this same verse to indicate the basis of this process. It is the "proper working of each individual part" that makes this process work (cf. 4:14).

Each member has a role to play in the church, adding something to the final growth of the body of Christ. This, Paul indicates, leads to causing "the growth of the body for the building up of itself in love." What is the significance of service? The significance of service is that believers grow spiritually and cause other believers to grow spiritually as well, as they serve one another.

The Mandate to the Ministry

At the heart of the mandate to the ministry is the Christian's responsibility to those who are in leadership over him, those who minister to him. Believers grow when given direction by spiritual leadership. Hebrews again provides us with a good passage that explains this truth. As the author of Hebrews closes out his epistle, he gives several exhortations for them to follow. One of these exhortations, Hebrews 13:17, deals with how Christians ought to respond to their leadership.

The author begins the verse with a general exhortation for the believers to whom he is writing to "obey" and "submit" to their leadership. For what purpose are believers to do this? The author gives a two-fold reason for this response. The first reason is because it is the responsibility of the leaders to guard or keep watch over the spiritual (soul) welfare of those in their charge. God has given to believers human role models who step in and, on His behalf, illustrate and teach what God wants them to be, while leading them in the process. This is why Peter reminds the elders that they are shepherds, and therefore responsible to the Chief Shepherd, Jesus Christ (1 Pet. 5:1-4). The second reason is tied to the first. The believer profits himself, if he allows his leaders to do their responsibility with joy rather than grief. It is profitable in that if the believer is not obedient and submissive, he will then come under the discipline of the church and God, which the leader would execute not with joy but with grief. Therefore, if a believer desires to grow in his life, he must properly respond to the spiritual leadership placed over him. This is the mandate to ministry for the believer.

Chapter Eleven
THE END TIMES AND THE ETERNAL STATE

"*For Isaiah spake thus concerning this space of a thousand years: 'For there shall be the new heaven and the new earth, and the former shall not be remembered, or come into their heart; but they shall find joy and gladness in it, which things I create. For, Behold, I make Jerusalem a rejoicing, and My people a joy; and I shall rejoice over Jerusalem, and be glad over My people. And the voice of weeping shall be no more heard in her, or the voice of crying. And there shall be no more there a person of immature years, or an old man who shall not fulfill his days. For the young man shall be an hundred years old; but the sinner who dies an hundred years old, he shall be accursed. And they shall build houses, and shall themselves inhabit them; and they shall plant vines, and shall themselves inhabit them; and they shall plant vines, and shall themselves eat the produce of them, and drink the wine. They shall not build, and others inhabit; they shall not plant, and others eat. For according* *to the days of the tree of life shall be the days of my people; the works of their toil shall abound. Mine elect shall not toil fruitlessly, or beget children to be cursed; for they shall be a seed righteous and blessed by the Lord, and their offspring with them. And it shall come to pass, that before they call I will hear; while they are still speaking, I shall say, What is it? Then shall the wolves and the lambs feed together, and the lion shall eat straw like the ox; but the serpent [shall eat] earth as bread. They shall not hurt or maltreat each other on the holy mountain, saith the Lord.' Now we have understood that the expression used among these words, `According to the days of the tree [of life] shall be the days of my people; the works of their toil shall abound,' obscurely predicts a thousand years. For as Adam was told that in the day he ate of the tree he would die, we know that he did not complete a thousand years. We have perceived, moreover, that the expression, `The day of the Lord is as a thousand years,' is connected with this subject. And further, there was a certain man with us, whose name was John, one of the apostles of Christ, who prophesied, by a revelation that was made to him, that those who believed in our Christ would dwell a thousand years in Jerusalem; and that thereafter the general, and, in short, the eternal resurrection and judgment of all men would likewise take place. Just as our Lord said, `They shall neither marry nor be given in marriage, but shall be equal to the angels, the children of the God of the resurrection.'"*[27]

DOCTRINE

Undoubtedly one of the most difficult areas for believers to comprehend and grasp is that of prophecy or end times studies. Its difficulty springs from several issues, such as, the difficulty of the images and language the Bible uses when covering these matters, the global nature of the topic (encompassing the whole spectrum of Biblical literature and time periods), as well as the futuristic nature of the whole discussion. As such we will not attempt to do a complete or exhaustive analysis of this area, but as usual will give an overview of the area focusing on the covenants as they relate to eschatology, the end times, and the eternal state.

The Covenants and Eschatology

An important part of understanding the end times is relationship of the biblical covenants to them. The covenants flow out of the historical events that define the opening chapters of the book of Genesis. These events can be understood by examining five key historical elements.

There are five historical elements which precede the biblical covenants. First, it was God's purpose to establish His rule on the earth through man (Gen. 1:26-28; 2:1-9, 15-17, 22-25). Second, man forfeited or gave up his right to rule to Satan (Gen. 3:1-21; Eph. 2:1-3). Third, God sought to establish His rule with mankind, but they repeatedly rejected Him, establishing cycles of offering of the rule of God and rejection of the rule of God. Fourth, God moved towards an individual, rather than all of mankind, to establish His rule through His unique personal interaction with him. To accomplish this, He set up several covenants throughout history, working all the covenants towards its (history's) culmination. Fifth, history is working towards the millennium. These five elements lead to the critical biblical covenants.

The covenants are the Abrahamic (general overarching), Davidic (expands the ruler and rule), and New Covenant (expands the ruled). Each of them plays a critical role in the plan of God.

In the Abrahamic Covenant, God separates a particular individual through whom to work. This is clearly indicated by the fact that thousands of years are covered in Genesis 1:1-11:32, then only three to four hundred years are covered in Genesis 12-51. God wants to emphasize the period of Abraham. There are three basic elements to the covenant: 1) land; 2) descendants; and 3) universal ramifications-king.

While there are several passages which contain the Abrahamic Covenant (Gen. 12:1-3, 7; 13:14-17; 17:1-21; 18:17-19; 22:15-18; Gal. 3:6-29; Rom. 4:1-25), probably the clearest Old Testament passage is found in Genesis 15:1-21. This passage emphasizes one key element about the nature of this covenant, its unilateral or unconditional nature. Meaning, it is not dependent on Abraham and his obedience for its fulfillment, but rather God Himself.

This is the major covenant from which the other covenants will proceed. The other covenants each expand an element of the Abrahamic covenant, further delineating it.

The second aspect of the Abrahamic Covenant to be expanded is the promise of a king. This covenant is called the Davidic Covenant, and, as the name indicates, was given to king David. There are three basic elements to the Davidic Covenant as well: 1) David's Seed; 2) David's Kingdom; and 3) David's Throne.

The covenant proper is mentioned and alluded to in several passages (1 Chron. 17:3-14; Jer. 22:1-5, 24-30; 23:1-6; 33:14-22; Lk. 1:30-33; Ac. 2:29-36; 3:18-26), however the major passages are 2 Samuel 7:4-16 and Psalm 89. Scripture indicates that regarding David's Seed (Descendant(s), he will not be disturbed again, he will build a temple, he will be chastened, God's permanent lovingkindness will rest on him, he will endure forever, and he will be a righteous branch (the first three clearly belong to Solomon, while the other three project the reader into the future).

Regarding David's Kingdom, the Scripture says it will be forever, God will establish it, and Judah and Israel will be regathered to inhabit it. Regarding David's Throne, God will establish it forever, and God will seat one of his (David's) descendants upon it. This covenant is also unilateral or unconditional. Nowhere in any of the passages is God's fulfilling of the covenant dependent on David's or his descendants' obedience.

The third aspect of the Abrahamic Covenant to be expanded is the promise of a seed or people. The New Covenant is called such because it is opposed to an old covenant. The Old Covenant is the Mosaic Covenant. The passages dealing with the New Covenant are numerous (Isa. 59:20-21; 32:37-42; Ezek. 11:17-21; 16:60-63; 36:24-34; Lk. 22:20; Rom. 11:25-27; 2 Cor. 3:2-18; Heb. 8:8-12; 9:15-18; 10:16-17;

12:23-24). The major texts that deal with the New Covenant are Jeremiah 31:31-34 and Ezekiel 37:21-28.

Several things are evident from the Jeremiah passage: 1) the New Covenant is made with Israel and Judah; 2) the New Covenant is not like the Mosaic Covenant; 3) because of the New Covenant, the law will be written in the heart; 4) because of the New Covenant, everyone under it will know God; and 5) because of the New Covenant, forgiveness of iniquity is possible.

Several things are evident from the Ezekiel passage: 1) based on the New Covenant, Israel will be regathered and live in the land; 2) based on the New Covenant, Israel and Judah will be made one nation with one king; 3) because of the New Covenant, there will be no more idol worship, but forgiveness; 4) based on the New Covenant, David will rule the regathered nation and there will be perfect obedience (see also 1:26-33); 5) the New Covenant will be a covenant of peace with Israel; and 6) based on the New Covenant, God will have his dwelling place with His people in the land. This covenant is also a unilateral covenant based on God who will cause the nation's obedience.

All three of the covenants culminate in the Millennium. The church fits into this program in that it is miraculously brought into the covenants by God incorporating the Gentiles into His chosen people. It receives, as do the Jews, the benefits because of its relationship with the Ruler of the future mediatorial kingdom (a kingdom mediated over by the vice regent), Jesus Christ, Israel, as its objects and Gentiles, as its recipients (Rom. 9:1-5; 11:11-32).

The End Times in General

The signal of the inauguration of the end times or last days was the resurrection and ascension of Christ and the descent of the Holy Spirit to indwell the body of Christ (Acts 2:14-21; Heb. 1:2; 1 Pet. 1:20; 4:7; 2 Pet. 3:1-13; 1 Jn. 2:18; Jude 17-21). However, the end times are also defined on a narrower basis as well, speaking to the events that will surround the summing up of human history (Mt. 24:1-13; Lk. 21:1-24; 1 Cor. 15:20-28). The following set of charts will attempt to explain the end times from both of these perspectives.

Eschatological Sequence of the End Times

There are several important areas within the above mentioned boundaries that should be noted. These are not exhaustive in nature, but are meant to give the believer a broad perspective on the sequence of the end times.

The Place of the Departed Dead in the Old Testament

Sheol or Hades was (and is still for the ungodly) that place of disembodied spirits/souls (immaterial part of man) (Gen. 37:35; Job 26:5-6; Ps. 88:10-11; 139:8). Both the righteous and the unrighteous went there after they died. The unrighteous to lower Hades and the righteous to upper Hades (that is, Paradise) (Lk. 16:19-31; 23:43).[28]

The Departed Dead After Christ's Resurrection

After Christ was crucified, He went to Sheol and liberated the righteous dead by transporting Paradise to heaven (Lk. 23:43; 2 Cor. 12:2-4; Eph. 4:7-10; 1 Pet. 3:18-22). Therefore, it can be said that for the Christian to be absent from the body is to be present with the Lord (Ac. 7:55, 59; Phil. 1:21-24; 2 Cor. 5:6-8; Heb. 12:22-23; Rev. 6:9-11; 7:9-17). At the time of Christ's resurrection, others were also resurrected to indicate the significance of the event (Mt. 27:50-54). These resurrections were different from restoration. This also gives an illustration of our resurrection (1 Cor. 15:20-24; 1 Jn. 3:1-3).

The Rapture

At the end of the church age Christ will come to meet His church in the air (1 Thess. 1:10; 4:16-17). The dead in Christ will rise first being given new bodies, and then we who are alive will be transformed into His glorious person (1 Cor. 15:50-57; 1 Thess. 4:13-18; 1 Jn. 3:1-3). This is not the second coming. At this time the church will be judged at the judgment seat of Christ, not for condemnation, as to salvation, but for rewards, as to service (2 Cor. 5:1-10). We will forever be with Him (Jn. 14:1-4; 1 Thess. 4:17).

The Second Coming of Christ

Once the church and its immediate Empowerer, the Holy Spirit, have been removed from the world, the wicked one (the Antichrist) will arise (2 Thess. 2:1-12). When he makes a covenant with Israel, this will commence the tribulation period lasting seven years (Dan. 9:24-27). Half-way through the tribulation, he will break covenant with Israel by setting himself up in the temple to be worshiped (Dan. 9:24-27; Mt. 24:15). He will begin persecuting Israel (Mt. 24:15-28).

At the end of the tribulation, Christ will return (Dan. 9:27; Mt. 24:29-31). This is the second coming (1 Thess. 5:1-11). The nations will gather for war and Christ will kill all the wicked, allowing only the righteous to enter the millennium (Zech. 14:1-11; Rev. 19:11-19). The Antichrist and his prophet will be cast into the lake of fire (hell) (Rev. 19:20-21). Satan will be bound for this period of time (Rev. 20:1-3). Believers will have returned with Christ to reign with Him (Rev. 20:4-6).

The Millennial Reign of Christ and the End of Time

However, since the righteous who entered the millennium from the tribulational time period are not in their glorified state, they can still produce children, who must also commit their lives to Christ. Not all do, as is the case now. However, there will be no open rebellion allowed in God's kingdom (Isa. 11:1-16; 65:17-25; Mic. 4:1-5; Rev. 2:27; 19:15). As a result there will many who will not be saved, yet still remain throughout the extent of Christ's reign.

At the end of the millennium, Satan will be released and will gather all the unsaved for one final assault on Christ (Rev. 20:7-8). He will be destroyed along with the other unsaved (Rev. 20:9-10). After this, all the wicked of all time will be resurrected and given immortal bodies. They will stand before the Great White Throne judgment for condemnation, and then be cast into hell with Hades, this is the second death (Rev. 20:11-15; Mt. 25:31-46). Afterwards, the New Heaven and Earth will be created after the Old Heaven and Earth are destroyed (Rev. 21:1-22:5; cf. 1 Corinthians 15:20-28; Matthew 25:31-46; Revelation 20:1-4).

Views of the Intermediate and Eternal State

Christians do not hold the market share on teaching regarding the eternal state. There are a vast number of different perspectives on the intermediate and eternal state. Since we do not live in a vacuum, it would do us well to know what these are, so that hearing them will not throw us off guard. Each of these views attempts to answer the question of what happens after death, but because they do not begin with the only religious leader, Jesus, to speak definitively upon it, these views fall horribly short.

One view of what takes place after death is called Annihilationism. Annihilationism teaches that man's soul is not eternal, and that the wicked who die are destroyed in hell. Punishment in hell simply means that the human soul is taken out of existence.

Another view of post-death experience is called Universalism. Universalism teaches that God will save all men ultimately. Hell is only for Satan and his angels, and not for mankind. Therefore, when those who are unsaved die, they will be brought into heaven also, and when they see Christ, they will accept Him. This is because God is love, and the atonement of Christ was universal (for all men) in its scope.

A third view of the state after one's death is called purgatory. The doctrine of purgatory is held by the Catholic Church. This doctrine teaches that upon death, believers are sent to a place of temporal torment at which time their venial sins are paid for. Venial sins being those sins that are lesser than mortal sins and therefore do not lead to separation from God in Hell. These venial sins could be such sins as abusive language or hatred that does not wish a person grave harm. After such payment is made, the believer is then allowed to go to heaven. One's time in purgatory may be shortened by one's service for the church, as well as the prayers of family and friends for that individual once he has gone there.

Yet a fourth view of this state is Reincarnation. Reincarnation teaches that the human soul is in a state of continual renewal. Upon death, the human soul is born again into another form. That form is dependent upon the positive life forces that person has generated throughout his life on the earth. One can be reincarnated in any form whether inanimate or animate, animal or human. The ultimate goal of this process is becoming one with the universe.

Each of these views of the eternal state falls short of what the Bible teaches on the eternal state. Both the Old Testament and the New Testament affirm that the eternal state is one of either eternal bliss or eternal punishment. Daniel 12:2 states that at the time of the resurrection, believers will be resurrected to everlasting life, and the unrighteous will be resurrected to "disgrace and everlasting contempt." Jesus repeats the same type of analysis of the eternal state in Matthew 25:31-46. Verse 46 says, "And these (unsaved) will go away into eternal punishment, but the righteous into eternal life." Jesus makes similar statements in John 5:25-29. Finally, Hebrews 9:27 indicates that mankind after death goes straight to judgment. That judgment then leads to his final assignment to heaven or hell.

APPLICATION

Hope is a very important aspect of the Christian life. The Christian finds himself in a situation in which much of that which is promised to him is future. While there certainly are benefits to believing in Christ that are evident in the here and now, it would be a skewed perspective that limits the believer's blessing or benefit to only life on this earth. As such, the Christian must be able to focus in on the future in order to operate properly in the here and now. No doubt this is the reason why the author of Hebrews states that "faith is the assurance of things **hoped for**, the conviction of things **not**

seen" (Heb. 11:1). It is clear from this verse that the undergirding virtue necessary for the effective living of the Christian life is faith. Faith itself is based on the virtue of hope. As we discussed in previous chapters, faith is that virtue that allows the Christian to take eternity and make it effective in the present. So, hope is important to the believer's walk. Two notable outgrowths of hope which we will discuss are: 1) hope and comfort; and 2) hope and steadfastness.

Hope and Comfort

The first outgrowth of hope that we will look at is comfort. By having the proper perspective on his future benefits in Christ, the Christian can experience comfort in his viewpoint on death. Death is truly the final and ultimate weapon of the devil (Heb. 2:14). Many a man and woman have been brought to their knees at the thought of it. However, the believer can draw comfort from his future in the face of the enemy of death.

In 1 Thessalonians 4:13-18, Paul teaches on the believer's future with Christ. His last verse in this passage reads, "Therefore comfort one another with these words." What are the words with which the believer is to be comforted? In this passage, Paul teaches several truths. First Paul sets the tone of the discussion by explaining that the believer's grief in the face of death is not the same as the person who does not know Christ. There is one primary reason for this Paul says. It is because the unbeliever has no hope (4:13).

After these words, Paul goes on to give two points regarding the believer's hope that enable him not to grieve as the wicked do. First, all believers who have died or who will die before Christ's rapture of His people will come with him when He returns to the earth (4:14). Second, those believers who have died before Christ's rapture hold a special place in the rapture of the Lord, and as such they will be united with new bodies, and join Christ in the air before those who are alive at His return (4:15-16). These truths, Paul comments, ought to be a comfort to the believer. By focusing on His future place with God, the believer can find the comfort of soul that he desires.

Hope and Steadfastness

Another important outgrowth of hope is that of steadfastness. In a similar form of exhortation as that found in 1 Thessalonians, Paul brings a section of Scripture to conclusion with the exhortation, "Therefore, my beloved brethren, be steadfast, immovable, always abounding in the work of the Lord, knowing that your toil is not in vain in the Lord." This exhortation comes at the close of 1 Corinthians 15:50-58 which focuses on the mysterious nature of the resurrection. What Paul says about the resurrection in this section of Scripture is important for every believer to understand.

In this section of Scripture Paul gives three major teachings regarding the believer's future resurrection. The first point that Paul makes clear is that a fundamental change must take place in humans to allow them to experience heaven

(15:50). This fundamental change has been provided for by God, however, and will take place at the sounding of the last trumpet when Christ comes to rapture His church out of the world. At this time the dead in Christ, as well as the living, shall receive new bodies (15:51-52; cf. 15: 35-49).

Paul's second teaching in this section is that God's plan for us has caused the believer to have victory over death. The victory of the believer over death takes the sting out of death (15:53-55).

Finally, Paul instructs the Corinthians that a response of thanksgiving is what the believer should have regarding these truths (15:57). It is very important to remember that the channel through whom we receive this victory is Jesus Christ Himself. Because of these important truths, the believer must "be steadfast, immovable, always abounding in the work of the Lord."

APPENDICES

APPENDIX 1

THE BIBLE'S AUTHENTICITY

INTEGRITY OF THE BIBLE

I. Internal evidence–what the Bible says about itself or evidence about itself
    A. Claims to be the Word of God or Truth
        1. 2 Timothy 3:16
        2. 2 Peter 1:20-21
        3. 1 Thessalonians 2:13
        4. 1 Corinthians 2:13
        5. Romans 3:2
        6. Hebrews 5:12
        7. Hebrews 1:1-2
    B. Inward consistency
        1. Multiple authors
            Over 35 human authors were involved in writing the Scriptures, yet all of the Bible is in agreement.
        2. Extended time
            The Bible was composed over a period of more than 1500 years, yet even with such a time span it evidences a great inward consistency.
        3. Varying audiences

There were a number of different audiences to which the Bible was written. Jews and Gentiles, bond and free, men and women, yet the message remained consistent to all parties.
4. Varying Skills
Each of the authors evidenced a varying level of skill. Some were skilled in Greek, others were not. Some were skilled in Hebrew, others were not. Yet even with this variance, God used each to express His message in a way that was congruent with the others who also wrote.
C. Progressive character
The Bible is an overall unit. Each part adds onto the other. The Old Testament is the seedbed of the New Testament. The New Testament draws on the Old Testament for much of its support (note all the times the New Testament quotes the Old Testament).

II. External evidence–what history says about the Bible
A. Acceptance by the church
Within 100 years of when the last book of the Bible was written, the church had begun the process of accepting the authority of all 66 books.

B. Manuscript evidence
Of all the ancient writings (ex. Homer's Iliad) the Bible has the most manuscript evidence (over 5000 manuscripts compared, for example, with the Iliad's 8). Yet other writings are more accepted than the Bible.

C. Preservation
For a text to remain without significant corruption evidences the special significance of that text.

D. Results
The Bible changes lives, and as such it must be a special book.

COMMON PROBLEMS WITH THE BIBLE ANSWERED

I. Miracles
    A. Exodus 14:21-30
    B. 1 Kings 17:15,16
    C. John 2:1-11
    D. Matthew 9:20-22
    E. Matthew 9:18-19
    F. John 6:16-21

II. Philosophy
    A. Ephesians 5:6-9

- B. Colossians 2:1-12; 2:23
- C. 1 Timothy 6:20-21

III. Other religions
- A. Deuteronomy 4:35-39
- B. John 10:1-11, 30
- C. John 14:6
- D. 1 Corinthians 8:1-6
- E. 1 Thessalonians 1:9

IV. The deity of Christ
- A. He is worshiped by men
    1. Matthew 2:11
    2. Matthew 14:33
- B. He is worshiped by angels
  Hebrews 1:6
- C. He is called God
  Hebrews 1:8
- D. Jesus claimed equality with God
    1. John 5:18
    2. John 10:30-33
- E. Jesus equated your attitude toward Him with your attitude toward God
    1. To know Him was to know God
        a. John 8:19
        b. John 14:7
    2. To see Him was to see God
        a. John 12:45

   b. John 14:9
  3. To believe in Him was to believe in God
   a. John 12:44
   b. John 14:1
  4. To receive Him was to receive God
   Mark 9:37
  5. To hate Him was to hate God
   John 15:23
F. Jesus gave power only God could give:
  1. To prophesy
   Matthew 7:22
  2. To cast out demons
   Matthew 7:22
  3. To perform many miracles
   Matthew 7:22

APPENDIX 2

OVERCOMING COMMON WEAKNESSES

I. General
1. 1 John 5:1-3, If we love God, we will be obedient
2. 1 John 5:4, You are able to obey because of your faith (Galatians 2:20)
3. Romans 7:15 - 8:11

II. Sexual immorality
1. Romans 13:13
2. 1 Thessalonians 4:3-8

III. Obedience to government & authority
1. Romans 13:1-7
2. Hebrews 13:17
3. Numbers 12:1-16
4. Numbers 16:1-50
5. 1 Peter 2:13-20

IV. Stewardship
Luke 16:10-12

V. Prayer
1. 1 Thessalonians 5:16-18
2. Colossians 4:2

3. Ephesians 6:18,19
4. Hebrews 13:18 (for leaders)
5. Luke 18:1-8
6. Luke 11:1-13

VI. Worry
1. Matthew 6:31-34
2. Philippians 4:6,7
3. 1 Peter 5:6,7

VII. Lack of respect for God
1. Hebrews 10:26-31
2. Hebrews 12:25-29
3. 1 Peter 1:17-19

VIII. Laziness, lack of discipline, or apathy
1. Revelation 3:15-17
2. Hebrews 3:12,13
3. John 15:6
4. Hebrews 6:7,8

IX. Humility
1. Proverbs 15:33; 16:19
2. Galatians 6:12
3. Philippians 2:1-11
4. 1 Peter 5:6-7

X. Gossip
    1. Proverbs 10:18; 11:13; 18:8; 20:19; 26:20-22
    2. James 4:11

XI. Lying
    1. Exodus 20:16
    2. Proverbs 12:19, 22
    3. Ephesians 4:25
    4. Colossians 3:9

XII. Unforgiveness
    1. Proverbs 17:9
    2. Matthew 5:23-25; 18:15-17, 21-35
    3. Luke 17:3-10
    4. Mark 11:25
    5. Ephesians 4:32
    6. Colossians 3:13
    7. 1 John 1:8-10

XIII. Resentment (Bitterness)
    1. Proverbs 26:24-26
    2. Hebrews 12:15

XIV. Anger
    1. Proverbs 14:17, 29; 15:1, 18; 16:32; 19:11; 20:3
    2. Ephesians 4:26-32
    3. James 1:19-20

XV. Envy
  1. Titus 3:3
  2. James 3:14-16
  3. 1 Peter 2:1
  4. Galatians 5:25-26

APPENDIX 3

STUDY AND DEVOTIONS

I. Pick a time
    A. Choose a time
        1. Ensure it is the same time everyday
        2. Ensure it is a time in which you will have the least amount of distractions (early a.m.; late p.m.)
            a. No phone calls
            b. No music or T.V.
            c. No childcare responsibilities
        3. Pray for understanding

II. Pick a passage
    B. Choose a book to study (i.e. Ephesians)
        1. Read the entire book in one sitting. If you do not read well, start by choosing a small book.
        2. Go back to the beginning of the book and determine what the first paragraph is. In most English Versions, the paragraphs are indicated by the beginning verse number of the paragraph being placed in bold text or being divided into paragraphs.

Paragraphs **do not** equal sections!
3. Pray again
Study the first paragraph
   a. Determine the major point of the paragraph
   b. Understand how the major point is developed in the paragraph.
   c. Write down your observations
4. Determine how you can become obedient to what you have learned or how you can apply it to your life.
5. Determine the second paragraph
6. Follow the same process as the first paragraph
7. Understand if/how the second paragraph is related to the first paragraph.
8. Continue this process until the entire book is complete. Study one paragraph a day (or week, etc.) depending on your desire.

C. Closing prayer
  1. Thanksgiving
  2. Confession
  3. Requests

D. Helpful Scriptures
John 14:26

APPENDIX THREE

IN-DEPTH STUDY

In using the Devotional Study approach given above, the following methodological approach should be of some assistance when attempting to gain deeper meaning of the particular passage that you are studying.

I. Observations: noting the details

In this area, the student of the Bible concerns himself with noting the important parts of the passage that he is studying. This stage is very important because it will properly prepare him for the following stage of interpretation.

A. Words

The words that are important will be apparent by noticing the ones that are repeated throughout the passage. Verbs are always important no matter how often they are repeated because communication is carried along by the use of verbs. At this point, the Bible student will make a list of the important words, as well as the verbs that are used in the passage he is studying.

B. Grammar

Each word, phrase, and clause should be defined as to its grammatical relationship within the sentence it is placed. Every word should be properly accounted for and placed in the broader scope of the author's thoughts. The grammatical ties should be clearly stated and noted on a separate sheet of paper.

C. Structure

The structure of the passage is also important because structure also carries the passage along from one point to the next. The Bible student should begin to make note of the connections between clauses, sentences, verses, paragraphs, and chapters, depending on the scope of his study. The important types of things he is looking for are the temporal relationships, cause and effect relationships, contrasts, comparisons, starting with general points and then working to specific points or vice versa, conditions, means, question and answer, proof or evidence, or analysis. Determine if any of these are a part of the passage that is being studied. A list of structural relationships and their verse parameters should be generated for the interpretation stage.

D. Literary form

Also important to the observation stage is the type of literature that is being studied. Is the passage poetry, prose, historical narrative, didactic (teaching style), prophetic, judicial (laws)? Each type of literature creates a different atmosphere. Each type of literature should be approached differently as well. For example, in a story the characters play a major role, thus careful observation of their characteristics is very important.

E. Atmosphere

The atmosphere of the particular literature that is being used should be noted. Where does the Bible student feel that he is as he is reading and studying the passage? Is he in a classroom, a court of law, or joining right in with the story itself? Each style of literature communicates a different type of atmosphere.

II. Interpretation: discovering the intended meaning

After the student of the Bible has taken careful note of what his passage contains, he must move to drawing significant meaning from those observations. Such meaning will come from piecing together the different elements of the observation stage.

A. Defining words, phrases and customs

The student must first properly define the key terms, phrases, and customs that appear in the passage being studied. The tools that will be used here are a good college dictionary, Bible dictionary, and theological dictionary. Each term or custom should be placed on a separate line with its own definition written next to it.

B. Uncovering underlying reasons and purposes

Here the concern is discovering if the author assumes that his audience has some particular knowledge already. Is there any assumed data? There should be a reason for everything that the author writes. He has carefully chosen his words and has said them in a deliberate fashion, therefore they are important to his meaning. What are his reasons or purposes for saying what he says? A reason or purpose for everything said in the passage should be written down on paper.

    C.   Drawing conclusions and implications

Can there be any conclusions or implications drawn from the definitions given, the reasons discovered, the grammatical relationships noted, the structural ties that have been isolated, the literary form in which the author presented the material, or the atmosphere that is created? If so, what are they? What is God saying through the human author to the audience he is writing?

III.   Application: determining the difference it makes in life

Once the passage has been interpreted to discover its meaning to its particular audience, the Bible student must then move on to apply it to his life.

    A.   Evaluate the relevance and value of the discovered principles

The first step in the application process is to determine whether there is an immediate application, or whether the principles must be sifted through time to make a clear application. All scripture is relevant, but the relevance may be indirect rather than direct.

B. Determine the kind of application: thoughts or deeds

What needs to be affected by this particular principle is the concern here. Is this principle calling for a change of thought? It may be corrective to what I think, or how I think. Is this principle calling for a change of action? Do I need to start doing something I am not doing, or do I need to stop doing something I am presently doing? Such a change may also include a change of thinking as well. The principle may also mean neither a change in thought or deed, because the principle may simply affirm what I am thinking or what I am doing presently.

C. Determine the area of application: where the principle applies

The focus here is a little different than the previous question. It deals with the sphere in which the application needs to take place. Possible spheres are the family, personal devotional life before God, relationships with other

Christians, relationships with the unsaved, speech, ministry, singleness, etc.
- D. Apply it

IV. Co-relationship: hearing the united voice of Scripture
- A. Compare with other Scripture (Special Revelation)

    Once the meaning of the passage has been determined, the results should be compared with other passages that deal with the same issue(s). This is also a checks and balances process to make sure that nothing outside of the scope of Scripture is wrongly concluded.

- B. Compare with experiences of life (General Revelation)

    Here the Bible student interfaces the Bible with real life. Ultimately life is dictated to by the Bible, but the Bible must be applied in the real issues of life.

- C. Compare with non-Christian ideas

    What do the unsaved have to say about this issue? Is there further insight that can be gained on why God says the things He says, based on what unbelievers affirm? That is, do God's words ring all the more true because of what the unsaved are thinking or doing?

APPENDIX 4

OVERCOMING HINDRANCES

I. Pleasures of Sin
    A. Practice self control
        1. Self control takes effort
           1 Corinthians 9:25-27
        2. Our confidence does not come from the flesh
           Philippians 3:1-8
        3. Our confidence comes from Christ
           a. Philippians 4:13
           b. Galatians 2:20
           c. Romans 8:1
    B. Practice renewing our minds
        1. Galatians 5:16
        2. Romans 12:2
        3. Ephesians 4:22-24

II. Doubt of God's ability to do what He said He would
    A. Jeremiah 32:17, 27
    B. Compare Isaiah 55:11 and Jeremiah 23:29

III. Disbelief in God's Word
    A. Flood–Genesis 7:17-8:1
    B. Sarah–Genesis 21:1-2

- C. Sodom & Gomorrah–Genesis 19:24
- D. Jericho–Joshua 6:2-24
- E. End of the world–2 Peter 3:1-8

IV. Unsettled surroundings/insecure place
- A. Maintain a divine perspective–Joseph (Genesis 45:1-15; 50:15-21)
- B. Maintain regimented spiritual disciplines–Daniel (Daniel 1:1-21; 6:1-15)
- C. Recognize the stability of God–David (Psalm 3; 18; 57)
- D. Focus on the internals, eternal, and the unseen–Paul (2 Cor. 4:16-18)

V. Impatience with God or others
- A. Constancy in prayer–Matthew 7:7-12
- B. Trusting in God's promise–see II. & III. above
- C. Greater love for people–1 Corinthians 13:4
- D. Greater growth in the Lord–Galatians 5:22-23; 2 Peter 1:5-7
- E. Recognize that you and God are on different schedules and thought patterns–Isaiah 55:8-9
- F. Have a forgiving rather than a condemning heart–Matthew 18:21-35

VI. Relationships
- A. Develop positive relationships–1 Corinthians 11:1; Proverbs 13:20; 14:9
- B. Do not associate with people who call themselves Christians, but live a contradictory lifestyle–1 Corinthians 5:9-13
- C. Avoid friendships with people who have a perpetual lifestyle of wickedness– Psalm 1; Proverbs 22:24-25; 23:20-21; 29:24; 1 Corinthians 15:33; Romans 16:17-18;
- D. Do not involve yourself in 50/50 contractual agreements with unbelievers–2 Corinthians 6:14-18
- E. Do not make your closest attachments unbelievers–2 Corinthians 6:14-18
- F. Avoid people who teach or practice religion at the expense of Christianity–2 Timothy 3:1-5; Romans 16:17-18

VII. No guarantee of outcome
- A. Obedience is the evidence of love–John 14:15; 15:10
- B. Recognize that the unseen is real–Hebrews 11:1; 2 Corinthians 4:18
- C. Trust God's Word–see II. & III. above

VIII. Fear of persecution or violence
- A. Recognize that persecution goes hand in hand with the Christian life–2 Timothy 3:12
- B. Do not be surprised at hardship–1 Peter 4:12-13
- C. Understand that others have experienced the same or worse–Romans 8:18; 1 Peter 4:17-19
- D. Focus on Christ's Suffering on your behalf–Philippians 3:10; 1 Peter 2:21-25; 1 Peter 4:12-19
- E. Realize that you are called to suffer–1 Peter 2:21

IX. Dealing with legalism
- A. It is impossible to please God without faith
  Hebrews 11:6
- B. God will perfect us
  1. Philippians 1:6
  2. 1 Peter 5:10
  3. 2 Corinthians 4:16
- C. God is at work in you
  Philippians 2:13
- D. Our salvation is begun and finished by faith
  Romans 1:17
  Ephesians 2:8-9

APPENDIX 5

ASSURANCE OF SALVATION

I. Through the work of God
   A. Salvation is **taken care of in eternity past for** the believer
      Ephesians 1:4-5
      Matthew 25:34
   B. Salvation is **based on God choosing** the believer
      Ephesians 1:4-5
      Romans 9:10-24
   C. Salvation is **a work of God in** the believer
      Philippians 2:13
      1 Corinthians 12:6
   D. Salvation is **carried out by God** in the believer
      2 Thessalonians 2:13
      1 Peter 1:1-2

II. Through a relationship with God
   A. Salvation **places** the believer **in Jesus' hand**
      John 10:25-30
   B. Salvation **places** the believer **in God's hand**
      John 10:25-30
   C. Salvation **seals** the believer **for God's future redemption**
      Ephesians 1:13-14

Ephesians 4:30
D. Salvation **promises** the believer **eternity with God**
John 6:40
John 10:25-28
John 17:1-3
Romans 10:1-13
E. Salvation **begins** in the believer **an unstoppable process**
Romans 8:28-30
1 Corinthians 15:50-58
1 Thessalonians 4:13-18

APPENDIX 6

DODGING DISTRACTIONS

I. Dealing with tribulations

The right focus is important in dealing with tribulations or suffering. Because of this, it is necessary to have four important focuses when you are in the midst of suffering.

    A.   Focus on the internals

God is at work in you to restore your spiritual strength day by day as you face struggles.

2 Corinthians 4:16
Philippians 2:13
Matthew 6:34

    B.   Focus on the eternal

God is going to reward you for faithfully withstanding tribulation. Tribulations here are not comparable to the glory that is to be experienced in heaven.

2 Corinthians 4:17
Romans 8:18

    C.   Focus on the unseen

This world and all that is in it is passing away, so the believer should focus on the eternal which will last forever.

2 Corinthians 4:18
Hebrews 11:1-16
2 Peter 3:10-13
- D. Focus on the spiritual benefits of suffering
  God uses suffering in the life of the believer in order to accomplish His ends of spiritual growth. This process starts with tribulation and ends with spiritual growth.
  Romans 5:3-5
  1 Peter 5:10
- E. Focus on Christ's suffering for you
  Christ has suffered for us, therefore we should be willing to suffer for Him, in fact we have been called to such.
  Hebrews 12:2
  1 Peter 2:21-25
  1 Peter 4:12-19

II. Dealing with relationships
- A. Do all in your power to maintain proper relationships
  Romans 12:18
  Ephesians 4:3
- B. Always pursue restoration when relationships are broken
  If someone has been offended or feels offended by you–Matthew 5:21-24

if someone offends you–Matthew 18:15-20; Galatians 6:1-5
C. Be sensitive (but not paranoid) to weaker brothers and sisters in the practice of your liberty
1 Corinthians 8-9
Romans 14
D. Be careful in making deep friendships and allegiances with unbelievers (see VI in Appendix 4, Overcoming Hindrances)
E. Maintain a good reputation before unbelievers
1 Timothy 3:7
1 Peter 2:11-12
1 Peter 3:13-17

APPENDIX 7

POSTSCRIPT ON THE HOLY SPIRIT

The doctrine of the Holy Spirit is a very volatile issue in the modern church era. It is one of the most debated areas of Christian doctrine between Christians themselves. For this reason, there are several competing ideas on who the Holy Spirit is, and what He was sent here to do. For this reason, it is important for us to have a good understanding of Him and His work, so that we will know error when we see it, even among our fellow Christians. This appendix will attempt to lay out for you a history of the doctrinal development of the church's understanding of the Holy Spirit, as well as to outline the meaning and use of spiritual gifts.

A BRIEF HISTORY OF THE DOCTRINE OF THE HOLY SPIRIT

Our approach in the historical section will be to look at the two major eras of doctrinal development. These eras are the Pre-Modern Era and the Modern Era.

Pre-Modern Era of Doctrinal Development

Christianity is essentially a dynamic relationship with God through Jesus Christ by the Holy Spirit which manifests itself (Christianity) through the combination of orthodoxy (right doctrine) and orthopraxy (right practice). It is proper maintenance of these two poles that marks authentic Christianity from religious imitation. In reference to the Holy Spirit, the focus of this brief history will be both His Nature (who He is) and His Actions (what He does). First, we will be looking at the Pre-Modern Era of Doctrinal Development, that is, the history of how the church has understood the Holy Spirit prior to the Modern Era.

The doctrine of the Holy Spirit is one of ten central doctrines that encompass the Christian faith. They are the doctrine of the Bible, God, Angels, Sin, Christ, Salvation, the Holy Spirit, the Church, and the End Times. Each of these doctrines developed at varying rates throughout the history of the church. This should not concern you, because it is the nature of doctrine that full formulation does not take without controversy. It is through dealing with erroneous views or with novel views on particular Christian doctrines or teachings that the church has found it necessary to clearly and precisely articulate what it believes and why. The development of the church's doctrine or understanding on the Holy Spirit has four distinct eras of development. Each era is characterized by a different level of unfolding and progress for the most part. These eras can be characterized as follows: I) Ancient Formulation; II) Medieval Neglect; III) Reformation Revision; and IV) Modern Eruption. The Modern Eruption will be covered by itself, since it is so extensive. The first three time periods will be examined first.

APPENDIX SEVEN

I. Ancient Formulation–AD 30-500

In the Ancient Formation of the church's understanding of the Person and Work of the Holy Spirit, His person (who He is) was the focus. While His work (what He does) was discussed in a rudimentary fashion, most pastors and theologians tended to focus themselves upon His nature. This is because there were many who were trying to teach that the Holy Spirit was not a member of the Godhead, that is, the Trinity, but rather the greatest creation of God. In the Ancient Church there existed an embryonic understanding of His person as being co-equal with the Father and the Son, as well as being the Empowerer of those who wrote the Scriptures and the divine Enabler. Of course, understanding during this period was greater than this in some areas of the church, but these are the essential elements.

II. Medieval Neglect–AD 600-1400

During the Medieval Era there was little to no advancement in the church's understanding of the Holy Spirit. This was an era of great stagnation in the history of the church with most of the time being spent on the codification of Christianity and not doctrine and life growing together. A particular aspect of the church's understanding of the Holy Spirit which was advanced during this time period was their understanding of the Holy Spirit as proceeding from both the Father and the

Son. This aspect of the Holy Spirit's relationship to the other members of the Trinity had been largely neglected during the Ancient Formation, not finding its way into any formal church wide doctrinal statement. While the Ancient Church recognized the Holy Spirit as proceeding from the Father, there was some confusion on the fact that He also proceeded from the Son.

III. Reformation Revision–AD 1400-1600

The Reformation Period was one of moderate to advanced moderate development in the church's understanding of the Holy Spirit. Both major reformers who fueled the development of the protestant church, to which we as a church are a part, Martin Luther and John Calvin, made major strides in articulating more clearly and more in-depth who the Holy Spirit is. As well as both strongly affirming and more clearly stating the co-equality of the Holy Spirit with the other members of the Trinity than did the ancient church, they also advanced in the understanding of His work. Major focuses regarding His work which they affirmed were: 1) His work in redeeming mankind; 2) His work in understanding the Scriptures–the doctrine of illumination; 3) His work in the progressive outworking of God's plan in the life of the believer–the doctrine of sanctification; and 4) His work in the affirmation of the Bible as God's Word.

From this brief survey it can be seen that our understanding of the Holy Spirit advanced throughout the existence of the church up through the 1600's. However, the articulation of many of His works and greater precision of the expression of His nature was yet to come in the modern era.

We will end this section with an early formulation of how the church of Jesus Christ understood the nature of the God it served. We would do well to take heed to its understanding. This is a creedal/doctrinal statement taken from the First Council of Constantinople in the year 381 at a gathering of church pastors and teachers, which was quoted in chapter seven. This doctrinal statement served as the stepping stone and the core for the church developing a clear and precise understanding of the person of the Holy Spirit.

> "We believe in one God, the Father Almighty, maker of heaven and earth and of all things visible and invisible. And in one Lord Jesus Christ, the only begotten Son of God, Begotten of his Father before all worlds, Light of Light, very God of very God, begotten not made, being of one substance with the Father, by whom all things were made. Who for us men and for our salvation came down from heaven and was incarnate by the Holy Ghost and the Virgin Mary, and was made man, and was crucified also for us under Pontius Pilate. He suffered

and was buried, and the third day he rose again according to the Scriptures, and ascended into heaven, and sitteth at the Right Hand of the Father. And he shall come again with glory to judge both the quick and the dead. Whose kingdom shall have no end.

And [we believe] in the Holy Ghost, the Lord and Giver-of-Life, who proceedeth from the Father, who with the Father and the Son together is worshiped and glorified, who spake by the prophets. And [we believe] in one, holy, Catholic (*Universal)* and Apostolic Church. We acknowledge one Baptism for the remission of sins, [and] we look for the resurrection of the dead and the life of the world to come. Amen." (Italics Added)

The Modern Era of Doctrinal Development or The Modern Eruption

In the previous section, we dealt with the first three eras of development. This section will deal with the final era, Modern Eruption. The Modern Eruption is divided into four periods: 1) Consolidation; 2) Neglect; 3) Explosion; and 4) Aftermath. Each of these time periods outline the distinct characteristic of the church's approach to the person and work of the Holy Spirit. Let us look at these four time periods:

I. The Period of Consolidation–AD 1600-1700

The period of consolidation occurred immediately following the Reformation Revision. The first generation of reformers had passed off the scene in the mid 1500's and the second and third generations expanded, enhanced, and propagated the Biblical teachings that had been reestablished by the Protestant Reformation. The Protestant Church expanded and with such expansion, its beliefs spread. The Protestant Church at this time policed itself, clearly condemning particular movements during this time period that tried to deny either His deity, His personhood, or His active work in believers' lives.

II. The Period of Neglect–AD 1700-1900

As is often the case with us as human beings, we tend towards the humanizing of our religious beliefs. This humanization appears in the form of a rationalism (a religion of the mind) or mysticism (a religion of the emotions). The eighteenth and nineteenth centuries were characterized by both. After the Great Awakening and stirring of Christianity of the Reformation, there began in the 1700's and 1800's deviant manifestations of Christianity. Rationalistic manifestations ignored the necessity of the Holy Spirit's work altogether. Mystic manifestations made the Holy Spirit into nothing more than a feeling or energy between God and man. However, both of these tendencies were avoided in many of the Protestant denominations.

In the properly balanced Protestant denominations, there was furtherance in the understanding of the Holy Spirit in reference to the Christian's life on the earth. The doctrine of sanctification was advanced, and greater discernment as to the believer's participation in the Holy Spirit's operation in man was affirmed in such men as John Owen, John Wesley, and George Whitfield. This was the era of the great evangelists who took the message of Jesus Christ all over the world, the first Great Awakening in America. Dependency of the Holy Spirit in evangelism was greatly affirmed.

III. The Period of Explosion–1900-1950

If the previous period was essentially characterized by neglect, it was just the calm before the storm. At the dawning of the twentieth century, a movement would be born that would forever change the church's understanding of the Holy Spirit. This movement would produce two other movements throughout this century. This movement is now known as Classical Pentecostalism.

Classical Pentecostalism grew out of the Holiness movement of the late nineteenth century, which in turn grew out of the Methodist movement of the mid-eighteenth to mid-nineteenth century. This was a movement tied essentially to the Holiness churches in

America, and was spawned by the supposed evidence of tongues speaking that centered around a man named Charles Parham, a Bible School president in Topeka, Kansas in the late 1890's. It was through this man's ministry that a black man nameed William J. Seymour converted to this new teaching and then sparked and fueled the Classical Pentecostal Movement (which would eventually become the most dominated Christian Movement of the twentieth century) in California, at the Azusa Street Methodist church, in Los Angeles.

This movement was characterized by a belief in two works of grace, one to get you saved, and the other to begin you on the track to sanctification, occurring sometime after salvation took place. Eventually the believer who has experienced these two works of grace would then experience a work of spiritual victory. These works would be accompanied by the sign gift of speaking in tongues. Such events as spontaneous group speaking in tongues, faith healing, exorcism of demons, etc. would characterize church meetings. Little control would have been exercised. While it was non-denominational it was very isolated in its effect. It essentially manifested itself in seven denominations: 1) Church of God (Cleveland, TN); 2) Pentecostal Holiness Church; 3) Church of God in Christ; 4) Assemblies of God; 5) Pentecostal Assemblies of the World; 6) United Pentecostal Church; and 7) International Church of the Foursquare Gospel.

Classical Pentecostalism gave birth to another movement that would take the quickly growing Pentecostal movement to places it had never been before with reference to mainline denominational churches. This movement would come to be known as the Neo-Pentecostal Movement or the Charismatic movement.

While the Classical Pentecostal Movement was essentially limited to denominations that tended to attract peoples of the lower socioeconomic strata, the Charismatic movement affected the middle to upper middle socioeconomic strata. The often reckless abandon of the Classical Pentecostal Movement was replaced with more subdued expression of tongues and the other charismatic gifts. This movement also viewed the revelatory process of God as still being open. In other words, the same type of revelation that God gave which formed the Bible through prophets and the apostles, can likewise be received today. This movement did not replace the Classical Pentecostalism, which survives today, but rather was an offshoot of the movement.

The Charismatic Movement was and is trans-denominational, which means that it might be encountered in any of the Protestant denominations or even the Catholic religion. Both of these movements emphasized and stressed the doctrine of the Holy Spirit to almost the detriment of all the other doctrines. This doctrine takes the predominate role in theology defining all other beliefs. The pendulum had swung to the other side.

IV. The Period of Aftermath–1960-

The church began to have to deal with this new teaching on how the Holy Spirit was to work during the Church Age. While the Classical Pentecostals could be ignored due to their existence for the most part in their own denomination, with the rise of the Charismatic Movement crossing all denominational lines, the teachings of the Pentecostal movement would have to be reckoned with. The person and doctrine that for so many years was either ignored or scantily dealt with by the church, now took the front seat. How would the church respond to how the Pentecostals understood the Holy Spirit to work?

Some took the low road and argued by character assassination. Others, however, took the high road and realized that many times our full understanding of truth only comes through conflict and debate. Thus, many Christians, pastors, theologians, and laymen returned to their Bible to look at why they believed what they believed about the Holy Spirit and how He worked. This produced a greater understanding of the Holy Spirit's Person and Work, and enabled the church to come to a much clearer perception of His work in their lives.

The debate still rages today. In the eighties, the Charismatic Movement gave birth to another movement called the Third Wave, or the Vineyard Movement, its chief proponent being John Wimber. This movement is attempting to erase much of the stigma of the Charismatic Movement as to its open ended policy on God giving new revelation today. However, it seems to be the same movement smoothed over. Christians continue to grapple with this movement's understanding of the Holy Spirit, answering it at every turn.

DISCERNING SPIRITUAL GIFTS

In our first division of this appendix, we looked at the history of the development of the doctrine and understanding of the Holy Spirit, as to His works and His nature. It is now time to look at the gifts of the Spirit and their usage. The concentration of our short study will not necessarily be an explanation of each gift, although a short definition of each is given, but rather to examine where the particular types of gifts are directed in their usage. We are unable to position each particular gift, so we will discuss them by grouping. There are a number of different grouping possibilities that are available when one is seeking to categorize the gifts, none of them are inspired. All the gifts are looked at as coming from Christ, through the Holy Spirit. Categories are to help us understand the gifts themselves as well as their usage. The category breakdown that will be used here is as follows: 1) The Service Gifts; 2) The Speaking Gifts; 3) The Servant Gifts; and 4) The Sign Gifts.

I. Service Gifts–Romans 12; 1 Corinthians 12-14; 1 Peter 4

There are eight gifts that fit under the category of the Service Gifts. These gifts are as follows: 1) Helps–the unusual capacity to serve faithfully behind the scenes, in practical ways to assist where needed; 2) Exhortation–the unusual capacity to either effectively urge one to pursue some course of conduct or to encourage or comfort one another in view of a past tragedy or trial; 3) Giving–the capacity to give of one's substance (food, clothes, money, houses, etc.) to the work of the Lord or to the people of God consistently and sacrificially with such wisdom and cheerfulness that others are encouraged and blessed; 4) Administration–the capacity to organize and administer with such efficiency and spirituality that projects are brought to a satisfactory conclusion with evident blessing; 5) Mercy–the capacity to do deeds of kindness, particularly to the undeserving or those passing through severe pressure or emotional anxiety; 6) Service–the unusual capacity to serve faithfully, extensively, and for protracted periods of time in a variety of different capacities and ways; 7)

Faith—an unusual capacity to see something that needs to be done and to believe God will do it through an individual even though it looks impossible; and 8) Distinguishing Spirits—the capacity to determine whether someone is speaking under the impulse of the Holy Spirit, his own human spirit, or evil spirits.

The Service Gifts are the largest singular set of gifts that are recorded in the New Testament. Their essential focus is for the edification of the body, that is, the common good of the body (1 Cor. 12:7; 14:12). As in the case of all the gifts, the Holy Spirit is their source, although they are practiced under the Lordship of Jesus Christ, and the careful outworking of God the Father Himself (1 Cor. 12:4-7). Each Christian has a specific function in the body of Christ, and is engifted in order to carry out that function (Rom. 12:3-4). The proper response to the Spirit's engifting is the vigorous enthusiastic exercise of the gift in the local body (Rom. 12:5-8). It will be noticed that almost all of the service gifts are qualities that every believer should exhibit. That which distinguishes these as spiritual gifts, is that there is an unusual capacity and or ability in the particular area to which is referred. In the local church such gifts as helps, administration, service, giving, and distinguishing spirits can effectively be used to work, enhance, augment, and greatly accentuate all its ministries. Someone who is engifted in this area, should choose a ministry in which they are interested and pour themselves into doing what is required to make it more effective through assisting and supporting. Those who have the gifts of exhortation, mercy, giving, and faith will find themselves fitting in quite nicely into such ministry areas that need encouragement and giving of time to meet needs. Such ministry areas as hospitality, comfort and care, etcetera, can be greatly enhanced by the person who is engifted in this area. Further, any ministry area can benefit from your participation in touching others' lives who need encouragement in their ministry areas.

II. Speaking Gifts–Romans 12:6-8; 1 Corinthians 12-14; 1 Peter 4:11

The next set of gifts that we will look at are those that fall in the area I have entitled Speaking Gifts. The speaking gifts are as follows: 1) Prophecy–the capacity to speak forth the truth of the Word of God to produce edification, exhortation, and consolation; 2) Teaching–a special capacity to understand and to communicate clearly the truth and application of the Word so others can learn and profit from it; 3) Wisdom–a special capacity for knowing and presenting the viewpoint of God and its relationship to the circumstances of life as presented in the Word of God; and 4) Knowledge–the ability to understand correctly the deep things of God as expressed through the Word of God.

The Speaking Gifts draw their name from their focus on the verbalization of God's Word in different contexts and in different capacities. Three of these gifts may have, in their manifestation or practice in the New Testament church (that is the age of the apostles), included at times new revelation from God on par with the Bible or have been part of the Bible. These gifts are the gift of prophecy, wisdom, and knowledge. Once the canon, the authoritative writing of the church (ie. the Bible), was completed, this aspect of these gifts was no longer needed, in that we have the complete, absolute revelation from God that He wanted His church to have (1 Tim. 3:16-4:4; Jude 3). Two of these gifts are also manifested in the Servant Gifts, yet are different from them. Both the gifts of prophecy and teaching are gifts independent of offices (that is, a specific position), yet are part of offices as well. This means a person who has the office of teacher in the local church has the gift of teaching, however not everyone who has the gift of teaching necessarily has the position of teacher or is meant to. It is the same for the gift of prophecy. It is evident by the categorizing of the gifts independently of the office (compare and contrast Rom. 12:6-8; 1 Cor. 12:4-11; 12:28-31; and Eph. 4:11). That which distinguishes the person with the gift from the person with the gift and office is that the person with the office receives a specific appointment from God (1 Cor. 12:28). This speaks to the specific commission or calling, as it were, to an official function or office in the local church, in most probability congruent with full-time ministry (cf. Jn. 15:16; Ac. 20:28–"made"; 1 Tim. 1:12; 2:7). Those who possess any of these four gifts will find themselves most aptly suited for the instructional ministry of a local body. Such ministry areas as a learning center, Sunday school, small group leaders, youth instruction, tutoring, and adult instructors are the ministries which will most benefit from your participation. Any ministry that is in need of insight or communication of truth from the Word of God is where a person engifted in this area can really make an impact.

III. Servant Gifts–Ephesians 4; 1 Corinthians 12

In the area of Servant Gifts there are five gifts or engifted people who are spoken of in Scripture. These five gifted types of people are: 1) Apostles–the authoritative position on establishing the practices and precepts for the church as the foundation for their being; 2) Prophets–the capacity to receive and speak forth truth which has been given by direct revelation from God; 3) Evangelists–the capacity to present the gospel with exceptional clarity so that people are persuaded to trust Christ; 4) Pastor(Shepherd)/Teachers–the capacity to shepherd the flock and provide clear spiritual nourishment for their Christian growth; and 5) Teachers–a keen interest in the personal study of the Word and in the capacity to communicate clearly the truth and application of the Word so others can learn and profit from it.

The Servant Gifts were mentioned earlier under point two. As was mentioned there, they tend to focus in upon a particular office or position in the local church or the program of God. God has given certain people as gifts to the church, as its servants (Eph. 4:7-11; compare 1 Cor. 12:28-31). Two of these gifts have ceased to exist in the local church and program of God due to their very nature. The Servant Gifts of Apostle and Prophet were given for the expressed purpose of building the foundation of the church (Eph. 2:20). Once the foundation was laid the gifts were no longer necessary. This is testified to in the New Testament due to the fact that we have no mention or record of apostles succeeding the first generation church, the apostolic church, either in the Bible or in church history. It is important to state here that this has nothing to do with God's ability or power to appoint such persons if He wills. What it speaks to is God's purposes. God is a God of order and as such He has purposes for what He does and how He does it (1 Cor. 14:33, 40). His purposes for giving the apostles and the prophets had to do with the foundation of the church and not the superstructure of it. Everything is to be built upon them. The other three gifts mentioned above are for the superstructure. They take what the Apostles and Prophets founded (that is, the truth in doctrine and practice that they passed on–Jude 3) and equip the saints in service, expressing this truth in their doctrinal beliefs and practices (Eph. 4:12-16). The person who is gifted in the areas of being an Evangelist, Pastor-Teacher, or Teacher best finds his expression in the leading, guiding, and overall shepherding of local bodies of believers or the assistance in such.

IV. Sign Gifts–1 Corinthians 12-14

The last area that we will examine is the area of Sign Gifts. Some refer to these as the Charismatic Gifts. In all, there are four gifts that fit in this area. They are: 1) Healing–the ability to heal all different types of diseases and illnesses; 2) Miracles–the ability to perform a broad variety of works of power that supercede the laws of nature, are outside the realm of God's usual working, and are only explainable by a divine intervention; 3) Tongues–the ability to speak in a language that has been previously unlearned for the purpose of presenting the gospel to non-Christians and to edify the church; and 4) Interpretation of Tongues–the ability to make intelligible and understandable what was hidden in the tongue or language that was spoken.

The Sign Gifts are probably the most debated area of all of the gifts in the modern day church. The nature of the debate is whether or not they are existent in the church today. Obviously, as in the case of the gift of the apostle and prophet, the question is not one of the power of God. He is clearly able to do as He has always done, if it is His will. The question centers upon the purposes of God. Is it God's purpose for the expression of these gifts in the modern church? This can only be answered if we come to an understanding of what the purpose of these gifts were. As we study the New Testament, there seems to be a three-fold purpose of the sign gifts: 1) they were to attest to the true nature of an apostle, prophet, or apostolic emissary, that is, they verified that the person doing the signs was in fact an apostle, prophet, or apostolic emissary (one directly appointed by an individual apostle or group of apostles to represent them for a specific reason); 2) they were to attest to the fact that what the person performing the sign was speaking was in fact direct and new revelation from God; and 3) they were to verify that a new era in God's program was beginning. Each of these purposes can be demonstrated from Scripture. First, their nature as validations of the person of an apostle, prophet, or apostolic emissary is taught in Scripture. It is clearly stated on numerous occasions (Ac. 6:8; Rom. 15:18-21; 2 Cor. 12:12; Heb. 2:1-4). In each of these passages, the author clearly teaches that God gave signs and wonders to validate the identity of a true apostle or prophet. Second, their function as a verification that the person performing the sign was giving direct and new revelation from God is also outlined in Scripture. Passages such as Acts 14:3 and 15:12; Romans 15:18-

21; Hebrews 2:1-4 show the integral tie between signs and wonders and their validation of the gospel message. They validated the new revelation that God was giving through the apostles and prophets. Third, Scripture also indicates that they were used to verify that a new era in God's program was beginning. The first half of the book of Acts is replete with signs and wonders. It is in this book that we have the historical progression of Christianity from a small Jewish sect to an all-encompassing religion with its own identity of beliefs. The giving of signs here are to indicate that this new era is being instituted. It validates that the new era is for the Jews (Ac. 2:1-13, 37-42), it validates that the new era is for the Gentile proselytes (Gentiles who had converted to Judaism (Ac. 10:1-48; 11:1-18), and it validates that the new era is for the Gentiles (testified to in the ministry of Paul and Barnabas–Ac. 15:1-12). One might wonder why there is such a need for these types of validating purposes. It is clear from Scripture that Satan has signs and wonders (2 Thess. 2:8-10). His signs and wonders, however, are for the purpose of deception, they are an attempt to deceive, which are **almost** good enough to fool the elect of God (Matt. 24:11; 15-28; 2 Thess. 2:10). One can see that signs and wonders would be very crucial in a transitional time to verify the different elements of that transition. However, once a complete form of revelation is available, the need for such signs and wonders would no longer be necessary, since all teaching, practice, and doctrine would have to conform with that unalterable standard.

I leave you with a portion of Paul's instructions regarding the practice of the gifts of the Spirit, "For just as we have many members in one body and all the members do not have the same function, so we, who are many, are one body in Christ, and individually members one of another. And since we have gifts that differ according to the grace given to us, let each exercise them accordingly . . ." (Rom. 12:4-6); for ". . . to each one is given the manifestation of the Spirit for the common good" (1 Cor. 12:7).

Works Cited

Athanasius of Alexandria. (1892). Festal Letters. In P. Schaff & H. Wace (Eds.), H. Burgess & J. Smith Payne (Trans.), *St. Athanasius: Select Works and Letters* (Vol. 4). New York: Christian Literature Company.

Augustine of Hippo. (1887). The Enchiridion. In P. Schaff (Ed.), J. F. Shaw (Trans.). *St. Augustin: On the Holy Trinity, Doctrinal Treatises, Moral Treatises* (Vol. 3). Buffalo, NY: Christian Literature Company.

Boston, Thomas. (1993). The Nature of Regeneration. In R. A. Torrey, A. C. Dixon and Others (Eds.), *The Fundamentals: A Testimony to the Truth* (Vol. 3). Grand Rapids; Baker Books.

Calvin, John and John McNeill (1960). Institutes of the Christian religion. (III, i, 1). In John Baille, John T. McNeill, and Henry P. Van Dusen (Eds.), *The Library of Christian Classics* (Vol. 20). Philadephia: The Westminister Press.

Hodge, A. A. (1998). *Outlines of Theology* (p. 300). Simpsonville, SC: Christian Classics Foundation.

Justin Martyr. (1885). Dialogue of Justin with Trypho, a Jew. In A. Roberts, J. Donaldson, & A. C. Coxe (Eds.). *The Apos-*

tolic Fathers with Justin Martyr and Irenaeus (Vol. 1). Buffalo, NY: Christian Literature Company.

Origen. (1885). De Principiis. In A. Roberts, J. Donaldson, & A. C. Coxe (Eds.), F. Crombie (Trans.) *Fathers of the Third Century: Tertullian, Part Fourth; Minucius Felix; Commodian; Origen, Parts First and Second* (Vol. 4). Buffalo, NY: Christian Literature Company.

Smith, M. H. (1996). *Westminster Confession of Faith* (electronic ed., p. 2). Greenville SC: Greenville Presbyterian Theological Seminary Press.

Tertullian. (1885). Against Praxeas. In A. Roberts, J. Donaldson, & A. C. Coxe (Eds.), P. Holmes (Trans.) *Latin Christianity: Its Founder, Tertullian* (Vol. 3). Buffalo, NY: Christian Literature Company.

Youngblood, R. F., Bruce, F. F., & Harrison, R. K., Thomas Nelson Publishers (Eds.). (1995). In *Nelson's new illustrated Bible Dictionary*. Nashville, TN: Thomas Nelson, Inc.

Endnotes

1. For a discussion of spiritual gifts please see appendix seven *"Postscript on The Holy Spirit."*

2. This is an excerpt from an Easter letter written by Athanasius, Bishop of Alexandria and defender of the faith, in A.D. 367, in which he defines what are the books accepted by the church of his day (Athanasius, Vol. 4, p. 551).

3. The audible voice of God was a limited occurrence within the Biblical record. Most of the occurrences of such took place surrounding the ministry of Moses. In fact, God made it clear to Moses that His normative method of communication with those who were to be His prophets would be through visions and dreams (Num. 12).

4. This rather lengthy quotation is taken from Tertullian's *"Against Praxeas,"* which was a defense of Christ's possession of two natures in one person. Tertullian, originator of the term "Trinity," which became the standard theological word to describe the Godhead, was born in Carthage in approximately A.D. 155. He was one of the greatest theologians of the ancient world, in many ways beginning the discipline which came to be known as theology (Tertullian, Vol. 3, p. 598).

5. Beget speaks of the special relationship between the Father and the Son; not that Christ had a beginning. See the discussion regarding Christ in the chapter entitled "The

Person and Work of Jesus Christ" for an explanation of this idea.

6. For a definition of these terms, please see the chapter entitled "The Basis and Means of Salvation".

7. This quote is taken from Origen's work entitled *On the Principles*. It is a work in which he expounds on differing Scriptures. They are exegetical in character. This particular section is taken from Book II, which discusses man and the material world. Origen is described in the Oxford Dictionary of the Christian Church as an Alexandrian Biblical critic, exegete, theologian, and spiritual writer. He lived from approximately A.D. 185-254 (Origen, Vol. 4, p. 287).

8. For a discussion on the assurance of salvation see appendix five.

9. This quote is taken from A.A. Hodge's *Outlines of Theology*, which has been called a detailed scientific analysis of Christianity. Hodge was born in 1823 to an academically oriented family, and was himself recognized as one of America's greatest theologians. He originally wrote this work for the laymen of his church, as a training manual given on Sunday evenings (Hodge, p. 300).

10. There is much debate related to the composition of the immaterial aspect of man and because of this, two different positions have surfaced: 1) trichotomy; and 2) dichotomy. Trichotomy says that man is made up of body, soul (conscious life), and spirit (spiritual life) (1 Thess. 5:23; Heb.

4:12). While these verses seem to divide the soul from the spirit, clearly a problem will arise from this view. Where do you stop? Since the Bible talks about the heart, mind, and other clearly non-physical entities, should we postulate a fourfold or fivefold division of man based on the body, soul, spirit, mind, heart, etc.? In fact, the immaterial aspect of man is referred to as the heart more than any other designation. In the passages in which soul and spirit are being used together, the authors are describing the immaterial aspect of man, not giving its composition. Man is a multifaceted, complex being comprised of material and immaterial aspect (Gen. 2:7; Eccl. 12:7; Mt. 10:28; Rev. 6:9).

11. You will notice that the terms know and knowledge are often used throughout the Bible to convey the idea of experience and not intellectual apprehension of something (Gen. 4:1; Num. 31:17; Jer. 24:7; 31:34; Mt. 26:72; 2 Thess. 1:8).

12. For a helpful discussion of ways in which believers can attain victory in the midst of temptations, refer to the appendices.

13. This quote is taken from a work entitled Enchiridion, written by Augustine, the Bishop of Hippo, born in A.D. 354. He is recognized by many as the greatest theologian of antiquity and one of the greatest Christianity ever produced. The work was meant as a Handbook of Christian Doctrine answering several questions with short answers posed to him by Laurentius (Augustine, Vol. 3, p. 246).

14. The particular focus of this verse is upon the sin of "unbelief." Unbelief is a sin that the believer must always fight against. This does not mean that due to backgrounds and makeup that each person does not have peculiar struggles unique to themselves.

15. This quote is the authoritative text of the *Nicene-Constantinople Creed* of A.D. 381, its form being accepted by the Protestant Churches. This creed is a slight expansion of the original *Nicene Creed* of A.D. 325, which was written by the bishops of that day who met at the city of Nice, to make an authoritative proclamation of the Christian faith (Youngblood, electronic ed., p. 2).

16. This reality is manifested by the fact that personal singular pronoun "I" is used by Christ, rather than "us" or "we" when referring to Himself (Mt. 5:21-48; Ac. 9:4-6, 15-16).

17. It is important to note at this point that when Christ became incarnate, He did not give up His divine attributes. This is important for a proper understanding of Philippians 2:5-11. To give up His attributes would mean that He would cease to be God. For example, can water still be water and not have the attributes of H_2O? Obviously not! Can someone be divine and not be all powerful? Obviously not! In becoming incarnate, Christ veiled the display of His divine attributes, although He continued to exercise His divine attributes.

ENDNOTES

18. For a discussion of this reality in the existence of Adam, see the chapter on "The Origin and Nature of Mankind."

19. The closest Biblical examples to this tri-fold office were Moses and Samuel. Moses was a priest (Ex. 6:16-20), a prophet (Num. 12:1-8; Deut. 34:10), and a national leader (Deut. 18:14-22; Num. 11:1-30; Heb. 3:1-6). Samuel was a priest (1 Chron. 6:27–28, 33–38), a prophet (1 Sam. 3:1-21), and a judge (1 Sam. 7:1-17).

20. For a discussion of God's ordination of the believer relative to salvation, refer to the chapter entitled *"The Basis and Means of Salvation."*

21. This quotation is taken from *"The Nature of Regeneration,"* one of the articles found in the Fundamentals, a 1917 work which attempted to defend the faith from the attack of theological liberalism and modernism. It was to stand as a testimony to the truth (Boston, Vol. 3, pgs. 130-132).

22. The hypostatic union refers to the union of two natures in one person. This is the opposite of the Trinity which is the union of three persons in one nature.

23. The word "atonement" does not appear in the New Testament. A basic search will reveal that most of its occurrences appear in Exodus, Leviticus and Numbers. There the believer discovers that man's sin could only be dealt with through sacrificial substitution and the shedding of blood (Lev. 1:4; 4:20; 7:7; 16:30; 17:11). This, of course,

previews the New Testament's teaching on Jesus' death without using the term itself (1 Pet. 3:18; 1:18-19). This has led to the use of the term to generally encapsulate what the Bible teaches about the doctrinal or theological content of Jesus' death.

24. The quote that opens this chapter is taken from John Calvin's Institutes of the Christian Religion. He was born in 1509 in Noyon, France and is the father of Reformed and Prebyterian doctrine and theology. Unrivaled as a theologian, pastor, teacher, and author, Calvin was one of the primary catalysts of the Protestant Reformation (Calvin, Vol. 1, pgs. 537-538).

25. See appendix 7 for a discussion regarding the nature and practice of spiritual gifts.

26. Taken from the 1647 Westminister Confession of Faith, penned by the Westminister Assembly on behalf of the English Parliament, this quote is part of the section on the church. The confession was written to help the parliament to restructure the Church of England according to Puritan teaching (Smith, electronic ed., p. 2).

27. The opening quote of this chapter is taken from Justin Martyr's "Dialogue with Trypho," a second century explanation of Christ being the Messiah of the Old Testament and the false position of the Jews in relationship to Christianity. Justin was born in Flavia Neapolis in approximately A.D. 114 (Justin Martyr, Vol. 1, p. 239).

28. It is important here that I indicate that the position stated in this section and the section, which follows, the relationship of the dead to Hades, is traditional, but not exclusive. It would be presented in the theological framework of John M. Frame (Frame, pgs. 911, 1077). But in the exegetical work of Bock and MacArthur, such a position would be rejected for paradise always being manifested in heaven.

www.ingramcontent.com/pod-product-compliance
Lightning Source LLC
Chambersburg PA
CBHW020924090426
42736CB00010B/1031